A HISTORY OF PEACE IN DAYTON OHIO

A HISTORY OF PEACE IN DAYTON OHIO

TAMMY NEWSOM

THE History PRESS

Published by The History Press
Charleston, SC
www.historypress.net

First published 2015

Manufactured in the United States

ISBN 978.1.46711.771.5

Library of Congress Control Number: 2015947038

To my family, whom I love very much.
To my dear son, Forrest. You are brave and smart, and I am very proud of you.
This is for Mom, Robin, Alan, Pat, Mary, Alex, Katie, Tommy and Chris.
This is also for my dad, Terry Keener. He lived peacefully.

CONTENTS

ACKNOWLEDGEMENTS

I wish to thank the following people and organizations for so generously offering their time, energy and knowledge in the creation of this book. Their work and focus gave me peace. Thank you to: Sarah Sidlow, Fred Arment, Steve Fryburg, Jerry Leggett, Felix Weil, Felix Garfunkel, Sam Lauber, Doug Keener, Kendra Mon, the Dayton International Peace Museum, PAX Dayton, Diana Keener, Robin Koebberling, Tom Walrab, Robbie Robinson, the Jewish Federation, Welcome Dayton, Matt Joseph, Irena Joseph, John McCance, Carl Westmoreland, Lisa O'Hearn, Kara Badgley, Krista Slavicek, Reverend Crystal Walker, Tariq Ahmad, David Yeh, G. Changa Freeman and Melissa Bertolo.

I would like to include a special note to Colonel Robbie Robinson: you inspired my son's class at school. Your experience was a powerful teacher.

INTRODUCTION

The United States government has a Department of Justice, a Department of the Interior and a Department of Labor. Why shouldn't it have a Department of Peacebuilding? In February 2013, Congresswoman Barbara Lee picked up the mission to introduce a Department of Peacebuilding into the U.S. government. She presented House bill HR 808 to Congress, called the "Department of Peacebuilding Act of 2013," to create a cabinet-level secretary position and the Department of Peacebuilding. Lee, like her predecessors, realized that to build an entirely new cabinet-level department demands a lifetime of dedication. Although this bill has been proposed to Congress some eighty-seven times since the days of the Founding Fathers in the 1700s, the recycled effort continues to gain popular support.

If such a department were created, it would possess the same magnitude and authority granted to any other U.S. department, such as the Department of Justice or the Department of Commerce. The term "peacebuilding" refers to activities that root out causes of violence as well as instill broad measures to prevent violent conflict and create sustainable peace.

In her web portal, Lee wrote: "The Department of Peacebuilding advances the good work of my friend and former colleague Congressman Kucinich (D, retired 2012) and has the potential to reduce suffering on a national and global scale while saving billions of dollars through violence reduction and increased economic productivity."

To attract legislative support for the bill, Kucinich defined and proposed legislation that would: one, hold peace as an organizing principle; two, endeavor to promote justice and democratic principles to expand human rights; and three, develop policies that promote national and international conflict prevention, nonviolent intervention, mediation, peaceful resolution of conflict and structured mediation of conflict.

Restorative Justice

Much of the legislation from the former Department of Peace bill has been passed as separate laws, including the Youth Promise Act. Many initiatives are still in the running. So without a winning vote, this is how the Department of Peacebuilding keeps going. The group attaches issues to larger proponents to propel peace forward. The most pressing aspect in the design of a Department of Peacebuilding is the call for restorative justice. In restorative justice, both the victim and the offender have a voice in the punitive system and in sentencing. Restorative justice is a 360-degree reparative approach to a criminal behavior that involves the victims and/or the victims' families, the perpetrators and the judicial and legal systems. Each party is given an opportunity to weigh in on the offender's sentencing, punishment and reform. In the following example, mediation between the victim's family and the offender was used as a low-cost alternative to punitive court costs:

> *There was an incident in a Florida penitentiary where a youth was convicted of murder. The victim's mother wanted to reach out to the mother of the offender because she wanted to meet the offender. The two families managed to do this, with no system in place for this to happen and the prison allowed that meeting to take place.*

"The reason for this is that there are victims at both ends of the gun. We are all responsible for creating a society so young people can go this route and take charge of their futures," said Kendra Mon. "The challenge here is—every day—every child deserves to be safe, loved and celebrated."

As a member of the Department of Peacebuilding Legislative Action Committee, Kendra Mon speculated on why the non-partisan legislation has not sufficiently caught lawmakers' attention. Congress has traditionally balked on passing legislation for an entire U.S. Department of Peace, she said, for a couple reasons: it would cost too much money to initiate, despite the long-term monetary benefits, and would promote redundant activities among the other departments.

Congresswoman Lee updated the agenda on the Department of Peacebuilding bill because of the "turf issue" between departments. "They took it from being a tug of war between the departments and chose to make it about coalition building," Mon said. The new HR 808 bill asked for programs that are covered under the other jurisdictions, such as the Department of Education or the attorney general's office, to be handed over to the Department of Peacebuilding. The revised bill called for peacebuilding initiatives in the federal government to repurpose legislation solely for a Department of Peacebuilding. The secretary of peace and Department of Peace would form coalitions and support programs by educating Americans about peacebuilding.

For example, the Department of Health already takes on violence as a community health issue, with a prescribed remedy of community education. However, with violent recidivism at a rate of 70 percent, the system just isn't working. The other problem is that Congress recognizes the Department of State as the acting Department of Peace.

"But that makes no sense," Mon said. "The Department of State deals with foreign and domestic governments. The Department of Peacebuilding is more than governmental initiatives." She continued:

> *The Peace Alliance is a non-governmental organization (NGO) that wants to dispatch trained peace-builders to supplement military initiatives. What we have seen in Iraq and Afghanistan is that now the military is asked to play two roles: one, go in and enforce a military action and two, conversely work as peacekeepers within the occupied communities to build peace.*
>
> *It is impractical for military to fulfill this obligation because it is hard to change hats. They don't have strength of training. Peace builders exist, and not just necessarily with the Peacealliance.org…Besides that, civilians don't trust peacekeepers that carry firearms.*

Congresswoman Lee's explained that the Department of Peacebuilding Legislative Action programs can be integrated into existing departments with little or no cost to taxpayers compared to what is already being spent on suppression of violence.

Lee issued this statement on her website:

> *This culture of violence that we live in is unacceptable. On our streets and across the globe, the pervasive presence of violence has infected the lives of millions, and it is far past time we address it as a nation. We invest hundreds of billions each year in the Pentagon, in war colleges, military academies, and our national defense universities all to develop war tactics and strategies. Now we need that kind of investment in peace and nonviolence here at home.*

According to the Centers for Disease Control and Prevention, each life cut short by a homicide costs the U.S. economy $1.65 million. Worldwide, the Institute for Economics and Peace estimates that violence and conflict cost the global economy $9 trillion in 2011.

"Lee and the peace action committees wanted to change the culture of the United States and the world to become peace-builders. Barbara Lee created the initial bill with Kucinich and then picked up the ball with HR 808 and called on her connections through the Peace Alliance to strengthen those initiatives and to make them stronger," Mon said. "Eighty percent of Kucinich's bill was aimed at gang violence, hate crimes and domestic violence. The bill covers education for humane treatment of animals and criminal reform. The Department of Peacebuilding would thus endeavor to become peace itself."

Until the Department of Peacebuilding is voted in, peacemakers have taken peace work to the community. Peace, Dayton.

1

ORIGINS OF PEACE, PRIDE AND PREJUDICE

Native American ancestors called the Ohio River Valley, the point where the five rivers meet, a synergized and sacred land. The Great Miami River and its tributaries—the Stillwater River, the Mad River, the Twin Valley River and Wolf Creek—provide a continuous flow of fresh running water, fertile plains and ample woods. A cavalcade of history has passed through this area from the late eighteenth century and on through the present.

Sometime between the late eighteenth and the mid-nineteenth centuries, the groups that had made Ohio their home discovered a way to make peace. Not by what they were given or where they were born, but they began to question how to improve their circumstances. These three groups were the indigenous native peoples, the white settlers and the slaves. Their destinies were intertwined and rife with conflict.

The first step toward peace in Dayton and Ohio was the advent of the Underground Railroad, an unofficial network of routes of travel, conductors and safe houses. The sole purpose of the Underground Railroad, or Freedom Trail, was to free the slaves. As Ohio became a state, one of the provisions was that the state was to be made free. Many who lived here in the North did not think that slavery should exist at all. This network was aided by settlers who abhorred slavery and by the other freed Africans who made the trek to freedom on the Freedom Trail.

A second alliance formed in the Miami Valley got results by using less risky tactics. The Warren County Peace Society, the second peace organization ever created in the world, was chartered in Springboro, Ohio, in 1815. The

An artist's print depiction of Tecumseh shielding colonial prisoners from other native attacks. *Courtesy of Virtue, Emmins & Co. Publisher, 1860.*

Peace Society also opposed slavery. By invoking the First Amendment, which guaranteed the right to free speech, freedom of the press and the right to peaceful assembly, the Peace Society published and distributed literature promoting peace, nonviolence and equality while speaking out against slavery. This forced the lawmakers to look in its direction and to respond directly to the challenges that America faced in becoming a truly free nation.

A third variable began to take shape while the first two groups fought nobly for a free nation: the plight of the Native Americans. Native Americans slowly disappeared from the tricot soon after colonial times. They fought bitterly against an unfair advantage and were wiped out after long and bloody battles with the white settlers and the English over custody of the land. They gave up office, as it were, to a stronger and more forceful legal system that did not protect their interests. Peace for indigenous peoples meant surrender to the colonists. Their culture and their numbers diminished.

Peace often runs parallel to war. For every battle fought and won in Ohio history, for every negotiation team sent to hostile territory, peace was the

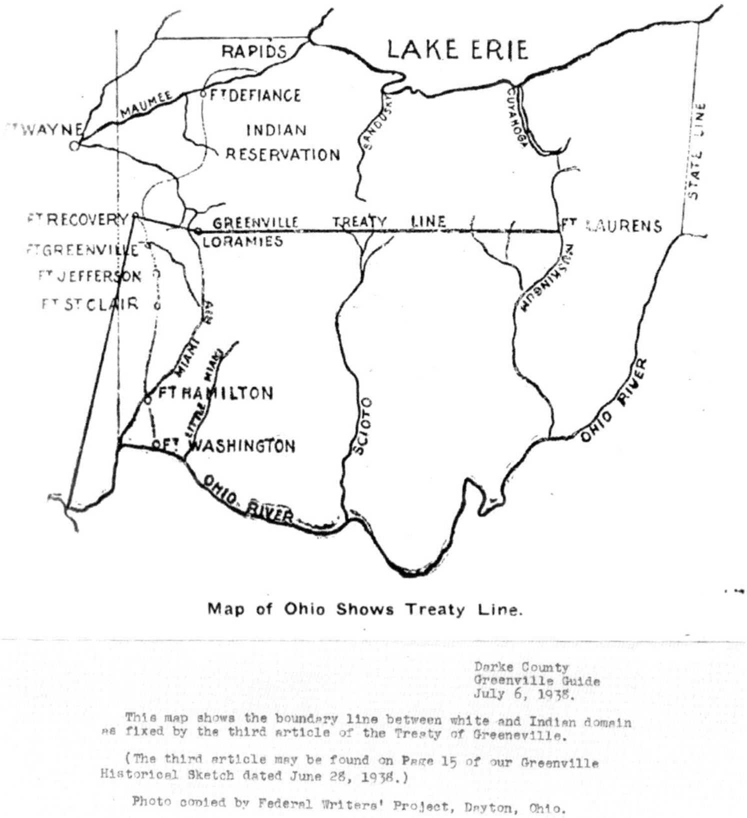

The 1812 map of the Treaty of Greenville line shows the native lands relegated to the Western Reserve. *Courtesy of the Federal Writers' Project, 1938.*

objective. Peace was not given; it was earned or taken. The settlers, the first groups to arrive in Ohio, had dreams of starting over in a free country, in a land free of religious persecution and ripe with opportunity.

Ohio Settlers

Second only to the Germans, the Irish made their mark on early Dayton history. The Scotch-Irish immigrants who arrived during the 1700s were prototypical frontiersmen. They were skilled with knives and guns, active, brave and loyal. Frontiersmen were also quick to drink or shoot, squat on landowners' property and exterminate any native person within sight. They settled in Montgomery County, with Dayton as the county seat, naming the area for Irishman General George Montgomery, a Revolutionary War hero. The first wave of German settlers emigrated from their homeland due to economic hardship and religious persecution. More than 75 percent of the immigrant population arriving in the territory between 1820 and 1860 were German born. These settlers were more liberal in their politics than the frontier colonists and more used to farming. These German immigrants were farmers, laborers, wagon makers and wheelwrights. Some of them were unemployed. They were not interested in protracted battles with either the British or the Native Americans.

Poorer families who could not afford the fare to voyage America would send their children instead. These children would be contracted into indentured servitude to pay off the debt and were guaranteed passage to freedom and a learned skill upon reaching adulthood. Indentured service contracts expired after a determined length of time. Since this was temporary servitude, most were able to buy their freedom with seven years of hard labor. Since there were no child labor laws to protect children until the twentieth century, youths aged six to sixteen composed the prime labor force in indentured servitude and worked the farms and kitchens of the Ohio country. Many of these indentured servants bound for Ohio were German settlers or foster children of German settlers who never saw their parents or siblings again, even after the period of service had ended.

In the book *The History of Mechanicsburg*, the stipulations of indentured servitude were made clear:

> *For all this labor, at the end of their servitude they were given a cheap Bible and a suit of clothes. Among the stipulations of the indenture, drawn up with great legal formality, the poor child was to receive each year six weeks of schooling.*[1]

Ohio was the seventeenth state admitted to the Union in 1803. A large portion of the German immigrants were Anabaptists—many of them Quaker, from the Church of the United Brethren in Christ Shakers or Dunkards.

There were several groups of German Anabaptist settlers who came to Ohio during this era. The Anabaptists, who were baptized as adults, wanted to be free to worship as they chose. The Amish, a subgroup, arrived in Ohio in the late eighteenth century. Ohio was seen as a mecca for religious pilgrims who could claim the land as their own. Ohio today has the largest Amish population in the world. Most Amish now reside in northeastern Ohio. Another group of Anabaptists, the Shakers—so named because they shake and quake when they pray—came to settle in Ohio in the early 1800s at the same time as the other Anabaptists groups. By 1889, many Ohio Shakers had already disbanded.

The most tenacious group of Anabaptists who left Europe in search of peaceful settlement was the Quakers. This group put its faith into practice. The Quakers started many peace groups, protested slavery and sought an end to war and violence. Not only did they want to be free to worship as they chose, but they also wanted to better the lives of those around them. The Quakers started several colleges in Ohio—many in Dayton and the surrounding southwest region—with the mindset of social activism and personal responsibility. Wilmington College, Wilberforce University and Antioch College in Yellow Springs have social justice and peacebuilding academic programs today.

Native Peoples

The American Congress wrote a few documents that ensured peace in America. Ohio country had first been organized for survey and sale after Congress enacted the Northwest Ordinance of 1787. The Northwest Ordinance provided organization and a government system for the territory northwest of the Ohio River. When Virginia conceded to give Ohio its own territory, slavery and indentured servitude were outlawed after 1800. Along with the prohibition of slavery, the provisions included promotion of education, morality and religion and the formation of three to five states out of the Northwest Territory. These new states were Michigan, Ohio and Indiana. To the north, beyond the mountains and beyond the Ohio River, was a new territory with an abundance of natural resources, and above all, it was free land.

After more than a year of talks, the British and Americans worked out a peace agreement. The Treaty of Paris was signed on September 3, 1783. The Treaty of Paris named the United States of America as a new nation, and Britain recognized its borders. The northern border became an imaginary line through the Great Lakes. The Mississippi River became the western border. The new nation stretched south to Spanish Florida.

With this victory, the British and American negotiators did include the Native American tribes who lived between the Appalachian Mountains and the Mississippi River. Some Native American tribes had been allies to the British. They hoped the British would win the war against the American colonists, who would be kept from moving beyond the Appalachian Mountains. To protect their own interests, the Native Americans formed the Western Confederacy, which included the Miamis, the Shawnees, the Wyandottes, the Mohicans and the Delawares. They were nations united to withstand American encroachment on their lands.

The British Empire ceded control of the Northwest Territory, which was occupied by numerous Native American tribes, to the United States but maintained many forts and outposts. Many Native Americans assisted in the expulsion of the English from the region; however, President George Washington directed the United States Army to halt the hostilities between the Native Americans and settlers and encouraged the enforcement of United States sovereignty over the territory. General Arthur St. Clair—from Marietta, Ohio's first settlement—was assigned to oppress native resistance on the western frontier.

General St. Clair discovered that Indians had attacked settlers from north of the Ohio River. On November 3, 1791, the Western Confederacy of Indian tribes, led by Shawnee chief Blue Jacket and Miami chief Little Turtle, defeated an American expedition of untrained recruits led by General St. Clair. The Western Confederacy, with minor supplication from the British, took control of the Northwest Territory. The engagement, known as the Battle of the Wabash, or St. Clair's Defeat, was the crowning achievement of Blue Jacket's military career and the most severe defeat ever inflicted on the United States by the Native Americans. There were 993 soldiers and militiamen killed. St. Clair was replaced by General Anthony Wayne because St. Clair had lost the battle. On August 20, 1794, Blue Jacket's Confederate army clashed one final time with Wayne at the Battle of Fallen Timbers, just south of present-day Toledo, Ohio. The land ultimately fell to the Americans.

General George Rogers Clark began taming the Ohio frontier in 1780 with the help of a military expedition from Kentucky. Clark returned in 1782 with one thousand men to square off against the Indians who had attempted to reclaim the territory. His efforts were successful in a skirmish at the mouth of the Miami on November 9, 1782. The present site of Dayton, the area was then called Venice, as the city was first named by Major Benjamin Stites.

The Treaty of Greenville was signed on August 3, 1795, at Fort Greenville, now Greenville, Ohio, thirty-five miles north of Dayton.

The land was purchased from John Cleve Symmes, a Revolutionary War soldier, to whom Congress had awarded the land. The purchasers were General Arthur St. Clair, governor of the Northwest Territory; General Jonathan Dayton; General James Wilkinson; and Colonel Israel Ludlow. Each of these new landowners came together to form a settlement named after General Dayton. A surveying team headed by Daniel C. Cooper then laid out a town site. The plan for central Dayton was to name streets for each of the other three.

At that time, the Native Americans were fighting in desperation to retain a foothold in Ohio. To avoid further conflict with the Indians and to out-muscle the Western Confederacy, Americans disregarded Native American claims to the land. Congress had been created, in part, to endow land-purchaser agreements to a select few, an arrangement that had become immoral to the natives. The whites were given carte blanche to land purchase agreements under the newly formed Congress. The British and French governments both owned American land tracts as well. These two countries would trade wartime services to both the Americans and the Indians in exchange for possession of the land.

The Western Confederacy was not aware, at first, that the Americans had won independence from Britain. Many forts continued to operate under English control due to debts that went largely unpaid. The native peoples fought, unaware that their land had been bought and sold from underneath them. The British landlords were forced out without reparation, and most Indian resistance was defeated by the time the War of 1812 was over.

The Northwest Indian War, which lasted from 1785 to 1795, ended with Battle of Fallen Timbers. By the end of the War of 1812, the native country in Ohio was all but extinct, as the United States gradually assimilated the boundaries over reserved land. In 1805, Blue Jacket—his native pride wounded but not his compassion—also signed the Treaty of Fort Industry to avoid spilling any more Shawnee blood. Although the Treaty of Fort Industry resulted in the gradual concession of more Shawnee tribal lands to the U.S. government, Blue Jacket knew he was defeated for the time being. When the treaty was signed, the Shawnee split off into three factions and fled to the Wabash River in eastern Indiana, some forty-five miles west of the Dayton area.

The Treaty of Greenville line that established Ohio as a state and opened western expansion began at the mouth of the Cuyahoga River, in present-day Cleveland, and ran south along the river to the portage between the Cuyahoga and Tuscarawas Rivers, in what is now known as the Portage lakes

An artist's print depiction of American soldiers sent to battle natives during the Battle of Tippecanoe, Indiana, circa 1811. *Courtesy of Kurtz and Allison, Print Publishers, 1889.*

area between Akron and Canton. The line continued down the Tuscarawas to Fort Laurens near present-day Bolivar. From there, the line ran west-southwest to near present-day Fort Laramie on a branch of the Great Miami River in Greenville. The line ran west-northwest to Fort Recovery on the Wabash River, near the present-day boundary between Ohio and Indiana. From Fort Recovery, the line ran south-southwest to the Ohio River at a point opposite the mouth of the Kentucky River in present-day Carrolton, Kentucky.[2]

Final attempts to reclaim the Ohio country came with the rise of Chief Tecumseh, Blue Jacket's successor. Blue Jacket was supportive of Tecumseh, who rose in 1811 to take up the banner in the Shawnee insurgence for lands in the Ohio country during the War of 1812. Rumors of Indian skirmishes along Lake Erie circulated, and war was declared on June 16, 1812, to repress this final coup. Legends sprung up around the charismatic Blue Jacket, who was supposedly a white man named Marmaduke Van Swearingen adopted by the Shawnee just before the Revolutionary War. Modern DNA testing proved the rumor to be false, but the legend was dramatized in the outdoor historical production *Blue Jacket*, produced annually in Xenia, Ohio, from 1981 to 2007.

For the seven years following the war, survivors on both sides roamed the countryside in search of wayfarers of the Western Confederacy and the white settlers but instead were met with powerful odors of death and destruction. At this time, there were no institutional arrangements for the handling of the dead in war conflicts.

Native conquest was made perfectly clear. As Frazer Wilson said in *Treaty of Greenville*:

> [Native Peoples] *wished Ohio to be a perpetual boundary of white and red men to the west, and would not sell a rod of the region north of the Ohio River. So Strong was this feeling that their young men could not be restrained from warfare upon the invading Long Knives, and thence resulted in the increasing attacks on the frontier stations and their emigrants.*[3]

Are You a Friend of a Friend? The Legacy of the Freedom Trail

Skilled enterprise knew no skin color: blacksmiths, farmers and tradesman alike were found both in the slave and free populations. The difference was a free man was paid for his labor and chose his place of employment; a slave did not. Many Ohioans, whether or not they belonged to a peace group, fought to change this iniquity. Dayton author and abolitionist Daniel Holmes published a dialogue on slavery in 1854:

> *Advancing sentiments too damning for to name, That Anglo-Saxons claim no legal right at all Over Ham's doomed race in servile bondage to enthrall, Would burst the bands and bid the slave pass out from under, From one who claims him as his lawful plunder. Appalling thought! May God forbid it ever shall that slave and master ever separate at all.*[4]

A network of old churches, college buildings and homes emerged as stations on the Freedom Trail. With twenty-three ports of entry along the riverfront and five important outlets along the lake, Ohio was the critical free state. The Underground Railroad, as it became known after the inception of the actual national railway system, ferried fugitive slaves to safety in the in the dead of night along a port on the north bank of the Ohio River and directed them to a route along which they were given a hiding place, food and a means of reaching the next station.

According to Stephen B. Weeks's 1896 study of the Underground Railroad, slaves probably used one of several routes to safety and freedom in the North. The first was the Kanawha road, which passed through mountainous areas of present-day Virginia and West Virginia to the falls of the Kanawha River and down that stream to the Ohio River, crossing at the present site of Gallipolis. Another option was the Kentucky road, which started at the western tip of Virginia then went through the Cumberland Gap and up through Kentucky to Cincinnati. The Magadee route was another road escaping slaves could take; it went over the Virginia turnpike, which ran from Richmond to the Ohio River at the mouth of the Kanawha River—a favored route from 1810 until the age of railroads. Many slaves crossed the Ohio River in the wintertime, even though the weather was harsh, because the river was too dangerous to swim across and had to be traveled while still frozen. The journey from the South to Canada took a full year.

The Underground Railroad itself was named for a slave who escaped to freedom in Ripley, southeast Ohio. To those pursuing the slave, it appeared as though he had just vanished or caught an Underground Railroad station. Soon, safe houses, or stations, began to pop up all over Ohio. The shortest route between Cincinnati and freedom in Canada was at the Lake of St. Mary's in Shelby County.

There were two routes into Montgomery County and seven routes out. The conductors on the Underground Railroad were not easily identified. The names of the conductors were often kept anonymous, lest they lose their property or get arrested. If discovered, the conductor could pay a maximum $10,000 fine and serve five years in prison. At the very least, if a conductor was identified, fugitives were barred from that station. Coded messages were often passed along to lead a fugitive to a safe house, map out an escape route or warn of suspected slave catchers in the area.

Personal satisfaction was the only reward in freeing a slave. Sometimes the law would aid in the rescue of a caught slave. Occasionally, a local magistrate or sheriff might look the other way if a slave was caught. If not, the slave could be returned to the owner or killed and the rescuer fined and imprisoned. Union Township in Miami County, Ohio—north of Dayton—was a Quaker settlement on the Underground Railroad network.

If a runaway was unsure of the safety of a station, he or she would knock on the door and ask, "Are you a friend of a friend?" This question was code

The Moses McKay house, built in 1818, was a known Underground Railroad station in Warren County in the late 1830s. *Courtesy of the Historic American Buildings Survey.*

for the fugitive trying to find safe haven. Quakers were known abolitionists who harbored fugitives on the way to Canada. Quakers went under the name the Society of Friends in the nineteenth century. So if the house was safe and clear, the owner of the house would reply, "Yes, I am a friend of a friend." Sometimes slaves were directed to safe routes and Freedom Trail stations from Western Ohio through to Canada by quilts hung out on fences or songs that mapped out the quest. "When the sun comes back and the first quail calls" was one such message.

Family histories of rumored Underground Railroad conductors were passed down through oral tradition. A well-to-do family of attorneys, the Kennedys of Montgomery County, was one such group of undercover abolitionists. The Kennedys owned the toll road on Frederick Pike and lived on the north side of the road crossing Needmore Road. This is near the present-day Drinking Gourd Music Store in Harrison Township, which was built in 1976. "Follow the Drinking Gourd" was a coded song that gave clues about the next safe house at certain times of the year.

The Kennedys' home, called Maplegrove, sheltered runaway slaves. The front porch of the home, now mortared stone and brick, was once made of wood, and it was believed that the slaves were hidden underneath it during the day.

As keepers of the toll road that ran beside their property, the Kennedys would shuttle conductors hiding fugitives to safety, toll free. Slave catchers, or those who were not known or trusted, were expected to pay the toll in full. According to historian Lisa O'Hearn, not many slave catchers went through Montgomery County or Dayton unless they were in pursuit of a particular runaway from farther south. Land was rural and, therefore, provided more places to hide, unless the law was tipped off. Most of the ex-slaves who decided to settle in town in the Dayton and Miami Valley area, once declared free, were relatively safe.

There are records of other abolitionists in Dayton who openly opposed slavery. Reverend Dr. Thomas E. Thomas, who assumed the post of pastor of the First Presbyterian Church of Dayton in April 1858, spoke out against slavery for three years before the Civil War. It was rare for an ecclesiastical church body to oppose the federal ruling on harboring fugitives in the antebellum South. Many northern Presbyterian churches were shut down for opposing slavery. The First Presbyterian Church prospered for thirteen years under Thomas's tutelage. The church embraced what was called the Pan-Presbyterian movement, which believed the law was not absolute and that God empowered men to be good stewards.

When the first shots of the Civil War were fired, Thomas said, "That rebel spark shall kindle a fire until our land is purified from the stain of the sin of slavery."[5] Other pastors who did not speak out against slavery at First Presbyterian did show compassion and fair and equal treatment to men and women, slave and free, in the congregation.

Mechanicsburg was the site of a story surrounding abolitionist Udna Hyde and his family; they resisted the fugitive slave laws to abet a fugitive to safety.

A runaway slave was able to buy his freedom with Hyde's help. Addison White ran away to Ohio, along the Underground Railroad, and made his way to Mechanicsburg—eighty-five miles north of Cincinnati and forty-eight miles east of Dayton. Addison hid in the Udna Hyde home and remained there for eight months, helping his rescuer recover from a broken ankle. White's owner, Daniel White, and three federal marshals eventually caught up with him at Hyde's home. Knowing the ruse was up, Hyde shouted to his daughter, Manda, in front of the marshals, "Feed the chickens, Manda! They haven't been fed this morning!"

Julia Williams Wadsworth, an ex-slave, settled in Medina. *Courtesy of the Federal Writers' Project.*

Nodding, she tore off outside. When she had a far enough head start, she began to run. One of the marshals called out after her, "Stop, girl, or I'll shoot!"

She hollered back, "Shoot and be durned!"

The marshals decided to let her go and then attempted to capture Addison White instead. White had barricaded himself in the loft of the log cabin with a loaded gun. One of the marshals known as Elliot discovered White hiding in the loft and climbed up the ladder after him. Addison fired a shot. The rifle ball struck Elliot's gun and ricocheted off the gun barrel, wounding his ear. White took off in a dead run.

"I am a dead man!" Elliot cried.

White was able to drive Elliot and the other two marshals away, but they soon returned. Armed with pitchforks and other weapons, the townsfolk arrived to help White and surrounded the barn. The townsfolk refused to let the marshals take the fugitive slave, whom they said fled to Canada in the scuffle. The marshals did arrest several people for aiding White in his escape, but they were released at the behest of the Clark County sheriff, who sided with the angry mob.

The marshals refused to release their detainees and proceeded to beat the sheriff and his posse. Eventually, another mob of Ohioans detained the marshals and jailed them in Springfield, Ohio, on the charge of assault with intent to kill, due to the altercation with the Clark County sheriff. Eventually, Ohio governor Salmon P. Chase negotiated the release of the federal prisoners and the marshals—all charges dropped. Daniel White tried to reclaim his slave. Mechanicsburg citizens raised $950 to purchase Addison White's freedom from his owner. Daniel White agreed to the sale.

Addison White enjoyed the remainder of his life as a free man in Mechanicsburg. He served two years in the Union army during the American Civil War. White was married to a free black woman in Kentucky. She refused to join her husband in Ohio, preferring to remain in Kentucky. Addison White eventually remarried.[6]

This story had a relatively happy ending. Other fugitives along the Freedom Trail were not so lucky. There was a sad story of a runaway slave who lived in Dayton, Ohio, for a few years until he was sent back to his former owner.

In *The Historical Collections of Ohio*, compiled by Henry Howe, the following story was reported in the *Dayton Journal* in 1832. The witness said a black man, going by the name of Thomas Mitchell, had lived in Dayton for two or three years. He was a hardworking and stable man, married and the father of a child. Some men from Kentucky arrested Mitchell and took him before a magistrate, claiming he was an escaped slave. The judge ruled they did not have sufficient proof and released Mitchell. The case again went before a magistrate. This time, new evidence was provided, and it was ruled that Mitchell was indeed the slave of the person claiming him.

Two young children, ex-slaves Isaac and Rosa, made their way to the farmlands of Ohio. *Courtesy of the Federal Writers' Project.*

A large sum was collected to buy his freedom. Mitchell himself gave fifty dollars from his own savings. The owner refused the deal and came to Dayton to take Mitchell back to Kentucky. When Mitchell met the man in the second story of a house and realized he was going to be taken, he tried to jump out of the window. He was restrained and forced to go with the man. Eventually, Mitchell did manage to escape. A man named Ben was taken to the slave owner in Mitchell's place as payment.

Later, a letter was received by a man in Dayton that told the rest of the story:

> *Poor Tom (Mitchell) Is Free Cincinnati, Jan. 24, 1832.*
> *Dear Sir:*
> *In compliance with a request of Mr. J. Deinkard, of Kentucky, I take my pen to inform you of the death of his black man Ben, whom he took in your place a few days ago…threw himself from the window…He was…severely injured and the poor fellow died this morning about four o'clock…Please tell Ben's wife of these circumstances…R.P. Simmons.*[7]

Although Ohio was a northern state and prohibited slavery, the state did little to interfere with the acquisition and the reclamation of runaway slaves. Oberlin in northern Ohio was the end port on the Freedom Trail. Oberlin was one of those towns where escaping slaves could feel safe, having arrived so close to Canada.

No Good Deed Goes Unpunished

The Fugitive Slave Law, signed by President Fillmore and enacted by the U.S. Congress in 1850, allowed federal marshals to arrest slaves who had escaped to the North and take them back to their southern owners. The law could arrest northerners suspected of aiding and abetting runaway slaves and imprison them or confiscate their land. This new law didn't deter the abolitionists. Many like-minded people secured a network to harbor a fugitive to freedom through Columbus and Zanesville to the east and Mechanicsburg and Urbana (fifteen miles to the west of Springfield) to the west. In southwestern Ohio, there were smaller communities that provided safety in an extremely dangerous territory for the escaping slaves. Chillicothe, Xenia and Hillsboro were notable communities assisting in this process.

Historians agree that rural farmers, as well as the Quakers, were instrumental in running and setting up the Underground Railroad throughout Ohio. However, there were relatively few abolitionists who stood up to the establishment as brazenly as Cincinnati Quaker Levi Coffin.

Levi Coffin and his wife, Catherine, were believed to have aided over three thousand slaves escaping over a period of years. For this reason, Levi was sometimes called the president of the Underground Railroad. The eight-room Indiana home they owned and used as a "station" before they moved to Cincinnati has been preserved and is now a National Historic Landmark in Fountain City, near Ohio's western boundary. Among the slaves who hid within it was "Eliza," whose story formed the basis for the character of the same name in the abolitionist novel *Uncle Tom's Cabin*. Coffin, at one point, was charged with four violations of the Fugitive Slave Act. His property was held up in court for $8,000.

The peace movement in Ohio organized long before the Civil War broke out. Peace groups were mainly religious societies formed with the intent of changing the government. These groups were empowered by the First Amendment: the right to free speech, freedom of the press and peaceful assembly.

Warren County Peace Society, 1815

In 1815, three peace societies sprung up independently in the United States. These peace societies were the first chartered peace groups in the world. In August of that year, the New York Peace Society was organized by David Low Dodge, a citizen and merchant of New York City, who acted as president. The second peace society was started in Springboro, Ohio, which is located at the northern point of Warren County, twenty miles south of Dayton. As many as four thousand slaves came through Springboro on the Freedom Trail. Springboro is listed on the National Register of Underground Railroad Stations. Nine houses in historic downtown Springboro are identified as Underground Railroad stations. Most of these houses are on South Main Street, at nearly the same spot where the Warren County (Ohio) Peace Society originated. The third peace society to form was the Massachusetts Peace Society (December 26, 1815), trained under the leadership of Noah Worcester of Cincinnati. Nearly a year later, the first European peace society began in England on

June 14, 1816. These societies were part of an organized movement based on religious conviction that war was inconsistent with the teachings of the New Testament of Christ.

Lodge wrote in his essays that any kind of carnal warfare is unlawful based upon Gospel principles. He wrote, "War is INHUMAN, UNWISE, and CRIMINAL, and whole genius of war is contrary to the spirit and precepts of the Gospel."[8]

The peace societies were concerned not only with abolishing slavery but also with the fate of the Native Americans. In *A Friend of Peace* (1815), Worcester wrote:

> *They may have some little excitement when they hear of savages—whose religion teaches them revenge—using the tomahawk and scalping knife; but when thousands are torn to pieces with shot and shells and butchered with polished steels, then it becomes a very polite and civil business, and those who perish are contemplated as only reclining on a bed of honor.*[9]

Less than a year later, Maine formed its own peace society. By 1817, twenty thousand copies of the pamphlet *The Custom Review of War* had been distributed by the London Peace Society. By 1828, fifty independent peace societies had sprung up all over the United States. Auxiliary peace societies,

This Quaker meetinghouse was built in the nineteenth century in Waynesville, Warren County. *Courtesy of the Historic American Buildings Survey, 1933.*

such as Promotion of Permanent and Universal Peace, were also gaining popularity during the early nineteenth century. William Allen, a London Quaker, assisted in creating its London chapter. The main objective of the many peace organizations was to capture the attention of lawmakers to introduce a change in legislation.

The Warren County Peace Society persisted in mailing out pamphlets to Presidents Thomas Jefferson and John Adams. Each president was petitioned by the Warren County Peace Society to establish a resistance to war and to abolished slavery. President Thomas Jefferson responded to pamphlets produced by Worcester, stating that "although gradual abolition of slavery was best…war cannot be compared to petty crime." John Adams responded to the same sample literature and pamphlets with some acrimony. "I do sir most humbly supplicate the theologians, the philosophers, and the politician to let me die in peace. I seek only repose." No president before Abraham Lincoln would voluntarily take a stand on abolition.

In the end, it was Congress that moved to abolish slavery by a two-thirds majority vote; ninety-three voted in favor, sixty-five opposed and twenty-three abstained to ratify the Thirteenth Amendment. It became unlawful to own slaves or to enslave human beings. Underneath the skin, man wears all the same color. The heart beats the same blood red. Upon whose trust is this diversity in kind given? If we want the world to look on what we have created, then the world is all love. We choose to be who we want to be, and we want to breathe free.

2

THE ERA OF INVENTION

Dayton became a city in 1805. After the British were evicted in 1812 and slavery was abolished half a century later, Daytonians became committed to creating an economically viable and more humanitarian city. Conscientious objectors within the region took personal responsibility to oppose war and violence. The Dayton age of invention brought the city national attention from the early 1900s.

A Dayton family built the greatest invention of modern man: controlled powered flight. Although the plane would be used generally for travel, sport and cargo, the Wright brothers held the belief that this invention would end all war. With close alliances to Charles Kettering, John Patterson, Edward Deeds and Paul Lawrence Dunbar, the Wrights became part of a tradition of Dayton inventors whose work had permanent and lasting effects. Inventor Charles Kettering once called the Dayton age of invention "a golden river: all you have to do is swim."

City of Dayton Established

At the start of western expansion, colonists flooded across the Alleghenies. With the admission of Ohio to the Union in 1803, Montgomery County was formed. The southern and eastern sections of the state were settled first, but the rich soil of the western farmlands soon attracted farmers who made it one of the garden spots of the nation. The county originally consisted of about 6,300 square miles, now known as the Miami Valley. Dayton was incorporated with a government of seven trustees acting as council, a supervisor and a marshal. Daniel Cooper became the city's first benefactor when he offered to purchase more than 3,000 acres of the land, including the site of the city, from Congress. Clear titles were passed to the individuals who settled here, and the first taxes, totaling $29.74, were collected from the twenty-two taxpayers in 1798. The first school opened in 1804; the first library society in 1805. The present school board system was beginning to take shape in the spring of 1806. The census of 1810 credited Dayton with a population of 383.

By 1812, Dayton had become a thriving town, complete with a new brick courthouse, five new taverns, grist and sawmills and frame houses replacing the pioneer log cabins. A nail factory, a dyeing plant, a weaving mill and a tannery were all in operation. Newcom's Tavern, in the modern-day Oregon District, is named after one of the original purchasers of Dayton land tracts.

Middletown, the halfway point between Dayton and Cincinnati, evolved into an industrial and entertainment complex, while a smaller settlement in the area, Germantown, maintained conservative policies to disallow the infusion of major retail chains or industry until the 1990s.

George Newcom's Tavern, erected in 1796, was named after one of Dayton's original twelve founders. *Courtesy of the Historic American Buildings Survey.*

From 1870 to 1911, Germantown's inverted bowstring, truss-covered bridge spanned Little Twin Creek on the Dayton Pike. *Courtesy of the Historic American Engineering Record.*

The community cauterized the village, which was founded by Phillip Gunkel and a majority German population. The villagers established their settlement in 1804. Germantown easily rivaled Dayton in size at its inception but did not grow past a certain point because the citizens wanted to prevent outsiders from influencing the establishment. Both communities, Dayton and Germantown, enjoyed the scenic view of the Miami Valley. Germantown's truss bridge, a covered bridge with an inverted bowstring design, was constructed in 1870 by the Southern Ohio Covered Bridge Association.

Neither Dayton nor Cincinnati saw the value in identifying their borders by their ethnic cores. The hope was that the population would become denser and more diverse as territory claims grew bolder. As the population of the United States became more diverse, so did the immigrant population in Dayton.

Wright Family Values

The Church of the United Brethren, which was similar to the Quakers, opposed war and violence. The Wrights, family of the famous brothers Wilbur and Orville, belonged to the Church of the Brethren. The Wright brothers, who built the world's first successful flying machine, believed their invention would put an end to war. They held steadfast to this philosophy throughout their careers.

Family of Entrepreneurs

In 1890, before the Wrights started building the airplane, they started up a couple of businesses. The first was a weekly paper, called *West Side News*, that was converted to a daily paper, the *Evening Item*, for four months. One of their printing clients was Paul Lawrence Dunbar. The Wrights printed the *Dayton Tattler*, a weekly newspaper that Dunbar edited. Dunbar was a high school friend and classmate of the Wrights. The Wrights ran out of new challenges with the printing business within a couple of years and closed up shop.

In 1892, the Wrights opened a second business, a bicycle shop called the Wright Cycle Company. At first, they busied themselves selling and repairing bicycles; Fleetwing, Warwick and Coventry bicycles were the top of the line of the day. Then, in 1896, they began to rebuild bicycles, which sold for twenty to sixty-five dollars each. The Wrights expanded on the bicycle repair services by adding a few original improvements to these customary components, including an oil-retaining wheel hub and coaster brakes, which are still used today.

Bicycles were the most technically advanced mode of transportation in the 1890s, but it was the possibility of manned flight that captivated the Wrights. When they read about the works of Otto Lilienthal, Octave Chanute and Samuel Pierpont, they were inspired to improve on their predecessors' areas of weakness. French inventor Clément Ader flew one machine more than 150 feet and only inches off the ground. He flew a second machine about ten feet off the ground. Using the same critical process they used to build, repair and improve previous bicycle inventors' designs, the Wrights advanced the designs of previous aviators, none of whom had achieved a successful manned powered flight. Without reinventing propulsion and effective wing shape, the Wrights determined the major folly was the pilot's lack of ability to balance and control the craft once it was airborne.

In 1900, the Wrights designed their first full-size, passenger-ready aircraft, once intended to use as a kite operated from ground control. This specialized craft was a bi-wing design—with two sets of wings, one above the other—and a framework that allowed their patented wing-warping process. This version had an elevator in front of the wings to control the angle of the aircraft, also known as the pitch.

Wilbur wrote to Octave Chanute and introduced Orville and himself. Chanute, then sixty-eight, was an established aviation pioneer. He had conducted his own flight experiments and documented the efforts of the many people who had attempted to build flying machines. Chanute became their good friend and encouraged Wilbur and Orville's efforts for many years.

When their design was nearly complete, they wrote to the U.S. Weather Bureau for help in locating the best place to build and test the plane. Kitty Hawk, North Carolina, had suitable wind conditions to conduct flight tests and the most plentiful sand dunes to cushion their landings if they crashed.

Wilbur and Orville left Dayton and resumed their experiments at Kitty Hawk on September 12, 1900, to begin assembling their seventeen-foot biplane. Their new kite/bi-wing had 165 square feet of wing area and a forward elevator for pitch control and some protection in the event of a crash. The first flights were made without a pilot on board. Without direct control of the plane from the air, the liftoffs were disappointing. On October 18, Wilbur climbed on board and flew the kite unbolted, for the first time, reaching 300 to 400 feet (91 to 121 meters) for up to fifteen seconds. They returned home with plans to come back to Kitty Hawk with an even larger glider.

Gliding and Wind Tunnel Experiments, 1901–02

In July of the following summer, the Wrights returned to Kitty Hawk at Kill Devil Hills, which is today the Wright Brothers National Memorial. They conducted tests with a new glider even larger than the one before—it had 290-square-foot wings. It also incorporated the foot-activated wing-warping control system that the pilot used to turn the aircraft. On a near miss that nearly cost Wilbur his life, they used Otto Lilienthal's calculations. A wind tunnel that breaks the sound barrier was developed as a way to test pitch, roll and yaw on an airplane without leaving the ground. Pitch, roll and yaw are the three factors that keep a plane airborne: front to back, side to side and vertical, respectively.

This glider was wrecked by a gust of wind during the Wrights' glider experiments in 1900. *From the papers of Wilbur and Orville Wright.*

The Race to Become First in Flight

Thursday, December 17, 1903, was the historic day of first flight. Winds of twenty-two to twenty-seven miles an hour blew from the north. The Wrights waited indoors until 10:00 a.m., when they decided to attempt a flight, fully realizing the difficulties and dangers of flying a relatively untried machine in high wind. The first successful flight ended suddenly; an updraft threw the plane down from a height of 120 feet in twelve seconds. In just a few seconds, the plane had clocked 6.8 miles an hour, with airspeed of 30 miles an hour.

Orville prepared for a second flight. Wilbur took his turn at 11:20 a.m. and flew about 175 feet in about twelve seconds. He also flew an up-and-down course, to test a similar pattern as the first flight, while operating the unfamiliar controls. The speed over the ground during the second flight was

Powered, manned flight was achieved at Kitty Hawk, North Carolina, in 1903. Orville operated the wing-warping mechanism. *From the papers of Wilbur and Orville Wright; courtesy of John T. Daniels.*

slightly faster than that of the first flight because the winds were diminishing. The airplane was carried back to the starting track and prepared for a third flight. There was no crash this time.

At 11:40 a.m., Orville made the third flight, tipping sideways with a gust of wind. Instinctively, Orville was able to warp the wingtips to recover and pointed the airplane down to land as quickly as possible. The new lateral-control wing warping was more effective than he had expected. The third flight lasted fifteen seconds and topped two hundred feet in the air before it struck the ground.

Wilbur started on the fourth flight at noon. The first few hundred feet were an up-and-down course similar to the first two flights. However, after reaching 300 feet in the air from the take-off point, the airplane was brought under control. The fourth flight reached a height of 852 feet over the ground and lasted for about fifty-nine seconds. Toward evening, using the dollar father Bishop Milton Wright had given them, the Wright boys sent a telegram:

> *Successful four flights Thursday morning all against twenty-one mile wind started from level with engine power alone average speed through air thirty-one miles longest 57 seconds inform press home Christmas.*
>
> —*Orville Wright*

Throughout 1904–05, the Wrights continued refining their piloting techniques and, thus, were woven into history's fabric forever as the patriarchs of manned powered flight. A third Wright Flyer was designed in 1905, in which Wilbur made a thirty-nine-minute, twenty-four-mile (thirty-nine-kilometer) nonstop circling flight on October 5. However, the 1903 Wright Flyer will forever be lauded in history as the first controlled powered airplane.

Katharine Wright

The Wright family stood behind Wilbur and Orville's undertaking, but it was their sister Katharine who was instrumental in getting the airplane out to the modern world. The Wrights had hired only one employee over the machine shop. They had a successful business but could not afford to hire employees to build the airplanes. Katharine recruited as many as fifty volunteers to help

Katharine Wright, donning aviator gear, is seated aboard the Wright Model HS airplane with her brother Orville in 1915. *From the papers of Wilbur and Orville Wright.*

with the heavy lifting and building of the gliders when the Wright brothers were competing and racing against other inventors for the patent rights.

Assuming the role of family matriarch at just fifteen when their mother, Susan, passed away from tuberculosis, Katharine also survived a younger sister who died in infancy. She was known affectionately by her brothers "Will" and "Orv" as "Sterchens" (German for sister). Milton, their father, was a bishop in the Church of the United Brethren, and Katharine was expected to host church functions in his absence as well as maintain household duties. Ever practical, Katharine hired teenaged housekeeper Carrie Kayler to help out so she could watch over the Wright Bicycle Shop.

Katharine graduated with a bachelor of arts degree from Oberlin in 1898, becoming the only Wright sibling to earn a college degree. She secured a job teaching first- and second-year Latin at Steele High School, a century-old Gothic building on Monument Avenue facing the Great Miami River in Dayton. Female teachers were often discouraged from teaching more complex or honors courses. The spotlight on the Wrights became

The Soldiers' Monument was erected on Monument Avenue in 1884. Steele High School, Dayton's first, was built next to it in 1906. *Courtesy of the Detroit Publishing Company.*

brighter, and the responsibilities of Katharine's unofficial position increased. Katharine enabled the family to continue to develop the airplane while she marketed the new invention. There were newspaper reports of her brothers' flights—which brought some notoriety—but the boys were uncomfortable with media attention.

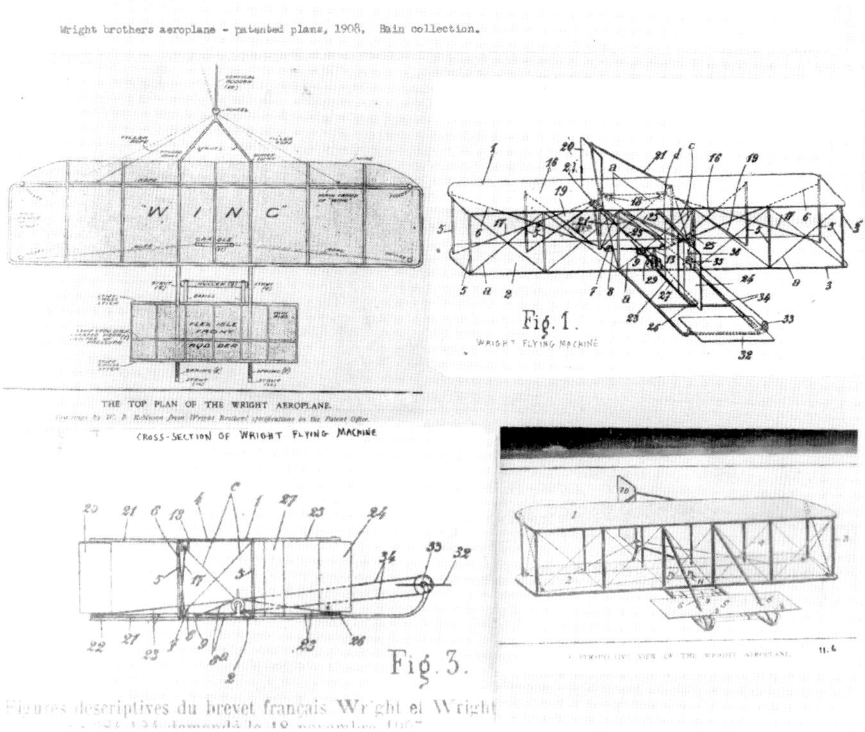

The Wrights shared detailed plans and sketches with their buyers during the marketing years from 1905 to 1909. *From the papers of Wilbur and Orville Wright, 1908.*

When the Wrights traveled to Europe in 1907, Katharine's social management skills of the business brought them to international fame. Her fashion of bunching up her skirts at the ankle, which enabled ladies to ride facing front on bicycles and horses, led to the invention of the "hobble" skirt.

Katharine stepped in as the social manager in 1908, and she continued to teach high school Latin. She met with kings and heads of state with little know-how of European protocol, but she won over the old aristocracy. The Wrights closed multiple high-dollar purchases upon demonstration.

Katharine made her first flights while in Europe. She was the third woman to fly in an airplane, after Teresa Peltier and Edith Berg, the wife of the Wrights' European business agent. Dedicated to her brothers' work, Katharine continued to serve as an ambassador for the family operation until her death at age fifty-four in 1929.

The Invention to End All War

In 1909, the Wright brothers sold their first airplane to the U.S. Army Signal Corps for $30,000. Their cost to build the plane was $6,000. The Wright Company was incorporated on November 22.

The notion that the airplane would put an end to war was widely held at the time. The airplane was an ideal instrument to conduct reconnaissance of enemy territory from the air with no loss of life. The pilot would only have to take pictures over the enemy lines and return with the documentation. Once the allied country had been made aware of the enemy's position and tactics, there would no longer be a need for prolonged battle. It would be impractical.

Dayton mayor Edward Burkhart, a Democrat, was reelected in 1909. His induction ceremony included a nod to the accomplishments of the Wright family. During his speech, the mayor presented the Wright brothers' medals as part of the celebration. "With the perfect development of the airplane, wars will be only an incident of past ages," Burkhart said.

A float in the parade that followed the presentations, sponsored by the West Side Business Men's Association, reiterated this theme with a banner

The Wrights' first airplane sale to the U.S. Army Signal Corps was recorded in 1909. *Courtesy of Harris and Ewing.*

that was emblazoned with the message: "The Wright Brothers' Invention Should Prevent Further Wars and Insure [*sic*] Peace."

Soon after the deal with the Army Signal Corps, the brothers sold their patents from the Wright Company for $100,000 and also received one-third of the shares in a $1 million stock issue and a 10 percent royalty on every airplane sold. This procured a bright financial future for their family's descendants and an unlimited set of possibilities for the world. However, a few unexpected events transpired.

With Wilbur as president and Orville as vice-president, the company set up a factory in Dayton and a flying school/test flight field at Huffman Prairie. The headquarters' office was in New York City. Surveillance and reconnaissance methods were how Wilbur and Orville were able to sell the plane to the Army Signal Corps. America had no close enemies and had no intention of going to war in Europe. Because Orville and Wilbur Wright believed a prolonged stalemate between nations of equal stature and economic status would be unwise and economically unsound, they extended their trust to their clients and nations that held the money and the means to develop peaceful applications for the airplane. The first overseas customers were the French, who didn't take long to develop weapons fired from the plane.

Wilbur passed away in 1912 of typhoid fever. Before 1915, when Orville left the Wright Company, he had sold a total of fourteen airplanes to the army.

The start of the First World War was sudden and eruptive. Infamous assassin Gavrilo Princip fired a single rifle shot that sealed the fate of Archduke Franz Ferdinand of Austria-Hungary on July 28, 1914. On April 6, 1917, America entered the conflict by declaring war on Germany. World War I incurred some of the most devastating losses in history: nine million military dead and seventeen million civilians.

During World War I, Orville was commissioned as a major in the aviation section of the Signal Officers Reserve Corps. He was assigned to work with the engineers at the Wright Company. The objective of the fledgling company went from the manufacture of a few sport planes to mass production of combat-ready aircraft. The company received a large contract from the government to build the British de Haviland DH-4 airplanes.

Orville believed the transformation of Dayton's own air invention into a weapon of mass destruction was not only inhumane but also impractical.

In a letter dated June 21, 1917, to C.H. Hitchcock in response to an aircraft program laid out by the Aircraft Production Board, Orville wrote:

A World War I *Dayton Daily News* cartoon warned, "The final settlement [for the Treaty of Versailles] must bring about justice to ensure permanent peace." *Courtesy of the* Dayton Daily News *archive, 1919.*

> *We thought governments would realize the impossibility of winning by surprise attacks, and that no country would enter into war with another of equal size when it knew that it would have to win by simply wearing out the enemy.*

Early in 1917, a group of Ohio investors, including Charles F. Kettering and Edward Deeds, president of the Dayton Engineering Laboratories Company, bought the Wright Company. Orville Wright lent his name and served as a consultant, but other than that, this was the only connection to the Wright brothers.

Kettering and Deeds's group was affectionately known as the Barn Gang. The gang developed its cutting-edge research on a farm in an undisclosed barn behind Deed's house. The Barn Gang's ambition was to make money on its prodigious inventions. Orville felt it was his duty to warn his clients of the dangers and futility of war, but once the airplane caught on, it was a byzantine effect that took on a life of its own. There wasn't any going back.

The Treaty of Versailles broke the bank of Germany. This financial rupture spurred a European nationalism that stopped thirty million people from living past World War II. Europe did not fully recover until the later part of the twentieth century. Kindness and generosity were all that was needed to sustain the mission of peace. The Triple Entente agreed to a cease-fire on November 11, 1918, ending the war in victory for the Allies. After the signing of the Treaty of Versailles on June 28, 1919, five years to the day after Archduke Ferdinand's assassination, Orville commented to a well-wisher, "The aeroplane has made war so terrible that I do not believe any country will again care to start a war."

3

NCR'S DESCH BOMBE AND THE HOLOCAUST REMEMBERED

By World War II, a sea of change had swept through the Miami Valley. Dayton had entered a progressive era. Believed by the Wright brothers to be the invention to end all war, the airplane pushed past the point of observation in military usage. An entirely new branch of the military emerged out of the U.S. Army Signal Corps: the United States Air Force. It formed in 1945, one month after the bombings of Nagasaki and Hiroshima. In 1948, Wright-Patterson Air Force Base (WPAFB), the Eighty-eighth Air Base Wing, was forged as a merger of Patterson and Wright Fields.

The drive toward westward migration was now replaced by technological expansion and a need to improve on what had already been done. With the goals of peace and prosperity, the National Cash Register (NCR) of Dayton was an example of one such company that broke the mold and saved millions of lives. During World War II, an NCR engineer and native Daytonian led the team that developed a new Nazi code–breaking machine that assisted the Allied victory in the Atlantic. As a response to the atrocities committed against innocent civilians and the cost of intense conflicts fought on two battlefronts, fifty-one countries joined together to form the United Nations in 1945. In 1948, a new law enacted by Congress granted displaced persons who had survived the Holocaust opportunity for permanent residency in the United States.

With the work of so few touching the lives of many, America's isolationist policies, firmly entrenched before the start of World War I, had become obsolete. As a world power, we were entrusted with global responsibility.

America and Dayton, Isolationist No More

In 1890, the United States Census Bureau declared that the American frontier no longer existed and therefore it would no longer track the westward migration of the population. Immigration to the Greater Dayton and Miami Valley regions had indeed slowed. Despite the enclaves of German settlers arriving throughout the nineteenth century, only 8 percent of residents in the Greater Dayton area in the 1890s were foreign born. Other more densely populated cities, like Chicago, had immigrant populations of 20 percent or more.

Although Dayton and the Miami Valley business community stayed small, its effects were far reaching. Dayton inventors, community activists, educators and innovators saw during this time a new and supplanted definition of peace. Dayton innovation and invention had national and international implications, which came about from the think-outside-the-box mentality and the dogged determination of the entrepreneur. Within thirty years, Dayton solely introduced the invention of the airplane, an improved automatic starter for the automobile, the invention of the cash register and the establishment of the Miami Conservancy District, which became a national model for dry reservoir construction and flood relief. Less than a century later, twenty-four Ohio astronauts flew into the space program, with Wapakoneta native Neil Armstrong becoming the first man to set foot on another celestial body.

When the Wright brothers' airplane reached European markets in 1908, travel and cargo transport, as well military applications, proliferated at home and abroad.

Staying true to his religious upbringing that air warfare was immoral and impractical, Orville was distressed at the use of bombs dropped on non-military targets. However, the invention of the airplane no longer belonged to two engineers from Dayton. This steel bird belonged to the world over. The first American passenger plane, the Ford Tri-Motor—also known as the "Tin Goose"—took to the skies in 1927. This three-engine plane, developed by the Ford Motor Company, was purchased by the U.S. Army Signal Corps. The Ford Tri-Motor proved useful in passenger, cargo and military installations.

France, the first importer of the airplane at the start of World War I, used the airplane for more than surveillance. The enemy camp, waiting for that signal scout to emerge, would want to put an end to the transmission of information back to the homefront. The peaceful objective of both sides of war fought in the air was to obtain aerial superiority—this minimized the risk of attack.

A new type of battle ensued. The aerial dogfight consisted of two or more fighter planes hovering above the earth, each clashing for aerial superiority. The pilots' skills required maneuverability plus agile use of the airplane and the calculated ability to shoot down enemy planes. Victory was ensured by cutting off the surveillance envoy sent out for reconnaissance. The dogfighters, capable of defending the reconnaissance team in times of surveillance, would also incite the third type of aeronautical vehicle, the bomber, which was developed for battle during World War I and World War II. Many of the original bomber designs created during the Second World War are still in use today.

Crash landings and fatalities became less frequent with the introduction of the parachute into the plane. In 1911, Grant Morton made the first parachute jump from an airplane, a Wright Flyer B, out of Venice, California.

Wilbur Wright passed away in 1912 due to prolonged illness. Orville Wright, who went on without his brother's support, seemed to shed more and more of his idealism as time passed. The use of the airplane in war had become more intense and purposeful, with greater destructive power. Orville felt it was his duty to train pilots on safety maneuvers and piloting techniques. A famous student of the Wright Flying School was Roy Brown, a Canadian who wanted to join the Royal Naval Air Service after graduating from high school. He needed a pilot's certificate, so he became one of the first pilots trained at the Wright Flying School through the Wrights' new army contract in 1909. Brown was credited for shooting down Captain Manfred von Richthofen, better known as the Red Baron.

The danger of civilian injury was much greater since a pilot could not see the final trajectory of a bomb dropped from the air.

In a letter dated August 1, 1917, to *New York Times* magazine editor Frank Harris, Wright expressed his concern regarding the safety of dropping bombs from the air without killing civilians. "In order to make bombing from aeroplanes effective, a vast number of planes would be required, and these well protected, so that the bombs could be dropped from a comparatively low height. Bombs dropped from a height of two miles or more rarely hit even near the mark for which they are intended." The tactical advice laid out in Orville's letter was incorporated into army air-bomb campaigns.

By 1943, after the United States had entered a world war for the second time, Orville Wright had become more resigned. In a letter sent on September 7 to Edward D. Smith, an executive with the NCR Corporation,

Orville wrote, "It was air power that made such a terrible war possible, but it also is air power that we will have to depend upon to stop it."

The early days of flight and aerial combat saw three types of airplanes that emerged. Later, over a dozen functions for the military aircraft were added and expanded upon, but the first types of military aircraft were reconnaissance aircraft, bombers and fighters. Reconnaissance aircraft are primarily used to gather intelligence or for surveillance. They are equipped with photographic, infrared, radar and television sensors. The second type is bombers, which are capable of carrying large payloads of bombs. Not as quick or agile as fighters, the bombers may sacrifice speed or maneuverability to maximize payload. The third group is fighters, which are used to establish and maintain air superiority. The fighters are agile and equipped to carry a variety of weapons, including machine guns and guided missiles.

Through the beginning years of World War II, America had provided volunteer aviator services to allies Great Britain and China, known as the Flying Tigers, and began developing an aeronautical arsenal, as the United States' inventory was supremely outnumbered by every country in Europe. Most of the early developments of military aircraft came from other countries because the United States stayed out of aerial conflict and the development of military aircraft until just before entering World War II.

The United States did not get involved in World War II until late 1940, when it was determined that Hitler may very well invade the United States after an open assault on the British during an offensive named Operation Sea Lion from 1939 to 1940. However, it was the Japanese that pulled America into World War II through Pearl Harbor. And it was the United States that had put the Japanese into an apocalyptic nightmare.

NCR and the Desch Bombe

In 1938, Edward Deeds, president of the NCR, hired Joe Desch, a brilliant electrical engineer, native Daytonian and University of Dayton graduate. Desch was optimistic, devoted to his family and possessed a strong work ethic. Soon after joining NCR, Desch had designed the world's first electronic calculator, using thousands of miniaturized gas tubes that could count one million pulses per second. A nonprofit agreement between the United States Navy and NCR launched the American code-breaking machine design contract, led by Desch. German U-boats threatened the security of Allied merchant ships. Disrupting the German U-boat submarines' Enigma transmissions became absolutely imperative to protecting the Allies' merchant ships and the seamen aboard them.

Beginning in 1941, NCR's Building 26 was turned into a top-secret factory with one thousand workers. Building 26, NCR's electronics laboratory, became home to the National Defense Research Committee, and Desch soon began working on top-secret navy projects there. Ultimately, Desch's research and leadership in Building 26 contributed to Allied victory in the Atlantic in World War II.

Desch hired two researchers, Louis DeRosa and Robert Mumma, and several other technicians to speed up production. Although these men were self-taught and lacked the university education Desch had, they were bright, curious and trustworthy. Together, the team produced applications and uses for the vacuum and gaseous tubes used in advanced electronics during World War II and beyond.

Famous British mathematician Alan Turing had designed a code-breaker for the Nazi Enigma transmissions at Bletchley Park in Milton Keynes, Buckinghamshire, the central site of the United Kingdom's Government Code and Cypher School (GC&CS). The invention was a "cribbing" system, a logical mathematical system for locating repeat strings of words used by the German military (such as "Heil Hitler").[10] Turing's ingenious code-breaking machine was called a bombe and enabled the British to read decoded German messages on the day they were issued. The efforts were brilliant, but the British did not have enough resources or manpower to keep up with the continual encryption and counterintelligence developed and enforced by the Nazis.

In February 1942, the German navy added a fourth rotor to its Enigma encryption machine. This expanded setting introduced more possible levels of code combinations in the Nazi Enigma system, and thus, it took long to break the codes. Unfortunately, this pushed the British code-breaking efforts at Bletchley Park further and further behind. Meanwhile, the undetected Nazi wolf packs were sinking millions of tons of Allied shipping and sending thousands of merchant seamen to their deaths on the ocean bottom. The technology for the cribbing system was not failsafe, and the chance that the Germans could induct new encryption methods to slow the Allies even further was equally apparent. In the case of the four-wheeled Enigma, it took Bletchley Park twenty-nine minutes for 336 possible combinations of letters for each phrase. Turing's team could take as much as four and a half days to decipher a single coded message. This brought unacceptable delays to the Allies' code-breaking efforts because it was not quick enough to warn seamen of approaching danger. The British, fearing a security breech, requested help from the Americans in building a more powerful code-breaking machine. Most British during World War II had never met an American and didn't know much about them.

The British feared American GIs couldn't keep a secret. However, the goings-on in NCR Building 26 was so secretive that no one knew who the real players were.

By 1942, Desch had been called in to engineer a short-timed delivery system on de-encrypting the German Enigma codes, beginning with reverse engineering superstar Turing's bombe design. The work was tense and never-ceasing, but Desch and his team had developed a few original innovations that the British adopted by war's end. Desch was determined to increase the efficiency and turn-around time of decryption. Solutions to increase expediency in decoding calculations were imposed by adding an extra wheel or rotor to enhance stop/start motion capabilities. This stop/start motion would read code at the point of recognition and would prevent the bombe from having to restart the decoding process at the beginning of the rotation—an ingenious yet simple solution.

A women's navy splinter group, the WAVES, was selected and brought in by the National Career Defense Institute (NDCI) to be trained at NCR on the use of Desch's bombes. The WAVES would begin the work of decoding the encryptions once the machines were built. The navy WAVES were trained in secret to solder thousands of delicate wiring connections at NCR's Sugarcamp before being dispatched by the navy to assemble projects at undisclosed work stations.

The official historian of World War II British Intelligence has written that it was the "Ultra"—the combined allied secret weapon developed at Bletchley Park and NCR—that shortened the war by two to four years. Without it, the outcome of the war would have been uncertain. Turing and his team were indeed credited as the theoretical masterminds behind breaking the German Enigma and Lorenz cipher codes. Bletchley Park is now an educational and historical attraction memorializing and celebrating those accomplishments.

When the NCR version of the bombes came on line in May 1943, the British acknowledged that the Desch bombes succeeded in deciphering code two to three times faster than the British version of the machine and were more reliably engineered. The British designed and built a total 200 bombes during World War II to intercept and decode Nazi U-boat communications under Turing's auspice. NCR built 120 machines under Desch's lead. The British ended up ordering 50 of those 120 machines for their agency's use and, by late 1943, ceded all the bombe work on the Enigma to the Americans.

Sworn to Secrecy

Like Turing, intense responsibility for the success in the Atlantic Theater depended on Desch's designs. Desch labored seven days a week yet was blamed by his navy supervisors for Allied losses every day his prototype machines were delayed. Turing also suffered under the strain.

Turing was persecuted due to his homosexuality and presumed to have committed suicide in 1954. Turing's death at age forty-one has since been reopened by the British government as a possible homicide. Desch, the son of a German immigrant mother and the nephew of a suspected Nazi sympathizer, suffered a different sort of persecution. Because of his German connections and because of the highly sensitive and classified nature of the work, Desch was placed under twenty-four-hour surveillance by a navy officer, Captain Ralph Meader, who was assigned to live in the same house with Desch and his wife, Dorothy, for the duration of the war. Desch was ordered to cut off all contact with his extended family at this time and with little explanation.

With security as tight as it was, the only person who ever compromised the navy project at NCR was James Martin Montgomery Jr., a third-shift lab employee in Building 26. Montgomery kept the navy and NCR guessing about the depth and latitude of his communications with the Nazis, as well as the nature of his loyalties during the war. He was from Franklin, Ohio, a paper mill town twenty miles south of Dayton.[11] When he was arrested, more than forty three- by five-inch index cards, scribbled with contacts from both Japan and Nazi Germany, were discovered in his vehicle. The navy didn't want the press to leak that Montgomery had committed possible espionage during the Desch bombe project.

However, Montgomery was never charged with espionage in his arrest. He was charged for stealing three non-gaseous tubes from NCR, valued at thirty-five dollars. He was detained in a federal reformatory in Chillicothe until the war was over. He was never fully prosecuted for espionage, and the reasoning for this strange legal consequence has raised speculation. Apparently, the navy would have rather risked espionage from a turncoat American than awaken the public to the nature of the activities at the laboratory.

While working on several Japanese codes in late 1944, Desch suffered from a mental breakdown and walked off the job. Although he was persuaded to return several weeks later, he was never quite the same. The navy's pressuring him to save lives and "bring the boys home" was overwhelming. Desch worked on several navy contracts throughout his thirty-five-year career at NCR. Although NCR was operating with other nonprofit contracts during World War II, the Naval Electronics Laboratory worked on the Geiger counter, which was developed for use on the atomic bomb without Desch's knowledge or consent. Desch had already walked off the job early in 1945. It was said that if he had known the real intent of the Dayton project, an official site of the Manhattan Project, he would have never come back. He did not find out about his role in the building of the atomic bomb until sometime later in the 1950s.

In 1940, two years after Desch started with the NCR, he met the aviation pioneer Orville Wright. As a devout Catholic, Desch struggled with his faith through the moral implications of war. He was under tremendous pressure because of the gravity of his research and was reminded daily of how many soldiers and civilians perished as the result of the war still going on.

As he and Wright climbed the steps together in Building 10, a bomber flew overhead. Orville had a limp by then, a result of a crash early in his career. Desch asked Orville if it bothered him that his invention has been used for war. "If we hadn't done it, somebody else would have," Orville said.[12]

In 1947, in a secret ceremony, Desch was awarded the highest civilian honor for wartime service, the Presidential Medal of Merit. Desch died in 1987 at age eighty, seven years before the project was declassified. President Truman honored Orville Wright with the Award of Merit for distinguished service to the National Advisory Committee for Aeronautics during World War II.

United Nations Created

Dayton benefitted economically from the war production, with $1.7 billion in government contracts. The newly formed United Nations, chartered in 1945, promoted peace as a benign sovereignty in cooperation with every nation as neighbors in obtaining prosperity, safety, quality of life and the use of military might as a necessity. All persons, regardless of age, race, nationality, creed or sex, are entitled to unbiased and equal treatment under the law. The UN was formed in coalition to protect displaced persons in direct response to the atrocities and crimes against humanity in Europe in World War II. The first group of refugees to benefit from the UN peacekeeping alliances and the Displaced Persons Act were the Jews.

The post–World War II boom saw a new wave of immigrants to the Miami Valley beginning in 1948. The Displaced Persons Act required the UN-participating nations to identify and protect persons in peril, with or without citizenship. Once a group of people are determined to be at risk and classified as refugees by the UN, they are guaranteed safe harbor until resettlement.

Before World War II started, Jews could still leave Nazi Germany. However, anti-Semitic sentiments had deep roots in other countries, which disallowed Jews to be admitted anywhere but Nazi-occupied territory. The Jews could leave Nazi-occupied territory, but they had nowhere else to go. Most were forced to return to the horrors of the death camps. The only country taking refugees prior to the start of World War II was England. The English government worked with rescue teams formed by German Quakers. They organized what was called the Kindertransport, a rescue effort that rescued and relocated children in peril before the war started. Once the Second World War began, no one was permitted to leave any Nazi-occupied territory. Defectors were killed crossing at every checkpoint.

Over 129,000 Jews immigrated to the United States from the late 1940s until 1952. The following are three Dayton-area residents who survived the Holocaust to settle in Dayton, Ohio. These survivors are our neighbors, our family, our co-workers and our community. These testimonies are relevant to Dayton's history because this is our community. Their testimonies are our education, and education is a key part of peace. The more we know, the less we err.

Holocaust Survivors Living in Dayton

Sam Lauber

Sam Lauber came to Dayton, Ohio, in 1998, after he was stationed in Manheim, Germany. He was assigned to work at WPAFB as a social worker and outreach programmer. He stayed on, rarely speaking about his Holocaust experiences, until he retired in 2010. As a hidden child, Lauber didn't realize he was a Holocaust survivor until he read that this group was the least recognized as Holocaust survivors. Between 10,000 and 100,000 Jewish children were hidden to avoid capture by the Third Reich.

Lauber was born in Antwerp, Belgium, in 1942, at the height of Nazi occupation in Europe. By this time, anti-Semitism was at an all-time high. Jewish children were mocked—not only by the other students but by teachers as well—as being physically and psychologically abnormal. Six million Jewish families and their children were systematically rounded up for transport to death camps or labor camps or executed on the spot. Most children did not survive encampment. However, fleeing the country during the height of wartime was very dangerous, and Belgium's borders were highly guarded from those refugees getting in and out of the country. Not to mention, few unoccupied countries would accept Jewish refugees. Many children, like Lauber, were hidden.

Until age three, Lauber lived with his family on Rue Gustav Fils in Brussels. Although the common language was Flemish, Sam spoke only French. Arranged by Belgian nuns and the church, Lauber was taken by his nineteen-year-old sister, Jenny, to live with a Christian family, the Detrys, in La Louvière. Lauber did not know anything about his newly adopted family, only that total and complete strangers had risked their lives or, at least, deportation to care for him and take him in as their own. There, he stayed as a member of the Detry family, regularly attending church as a Christian boy, going out to school and on shopping trips. He soon bonded with the Detrys' own son, Jean Marie, who was about his age. After a year, his sister, Jenny, returned for him, and he was reunited with his parents, who had survived.

Lauber was told to blend in with his surroundings, pretend like he was at camp and play like a good little boy until they came back to the Detrys' to bring him home. After six years together in Belgium, the family planned a move to the United States in 1948. Lauber's parents had relatives in New York City and Detroit. They could no longer stay in Belgium, where they had lost all of their possessions. They longed for a fresh start, and the United States loomed large and golden as a free country and a land of opportunity. Lauber became an automatic United States citizen in 1954–55.

By 1957, Lauber's mother had passed away, and three years later, his father did too. His parents had been very ill because of the war. Lauber joined the U.S. Army and, later, got married and adopted a son. But for many years, he wondered about the family who had taken him in as a total stranger.

In 1986, while stationed as a civilian at Dusseldorf, Lauber decided to return to La Louvière with his wife and son to reconnect with the family that saved his life. Having found their phone number, he called the household. Madame Detry answered, "Dede (pronounced "Duh-Day"), is that you?" He had stayed with them for only a year and half, but the Detrys remembered the nickname they had given him as if it were yesterday.

After a seventeen-year tour of service in Germany, Lauber decided he wanted to speak out and share his experiences with other survivors. Across the nation, the history of the Holocaust and its remembrance touches all. Lauber's story has appeared in two books, including a Holocaust survivor cookbook. His picture and biography can be found at the Museum of the United States Air Force Holocaust exhibit "Prejudice and Memory." In 1991, the Anti-Defamation League came to New York to organize a conference of former hidden children who survived the Nazis. Lauber has attended many such functions. His sister lives in Florida, and his son lives in Indianapolis.

Felix Weil

Felix Weil was born in Germany in 1927 and was moved to England, away from his family, in 1939. The war had not yet started, and Germany's borders were safe to cross to find a safe house to wait out Nazi occupation, which had begun in 1933. Through the Quaker-sanctioned rescue operation Kindertransport, Weil was among the children rescued from Austria and Czechoslovakia. The Kindertransport was first come, first served, and Weil was put on a waiting list at age eleven. One and a half million Jewish children were murdered during World War II, and he was but one of the ten thousand saved.

"At the time just prior it was quite impossible to leave Nazi Germany unless you were a direct target but nearly impossible to go to the Nazi annex of Austria," said Weil. "Any Jewish person was welcome to leave Germany, but England was the only country that would take them in as refugees. The U.S. had closed its borders due to overflowing quotas."

In 1939, Weil was taken to England, as were the other children from the Kindertransport.

"I felt very fortunate to be on that list of 10,000 children," Weil said. He found out after that his parents and sister all perished in the concentration camps. He was hidden in England until 1941, as no letters mailed out arrived in Germany, and none from Germany were sent out to England, while the countries were at war. He had not heard of his family's plight. Although Weil continued to write letters, hoping to reach home, he was taken in by a

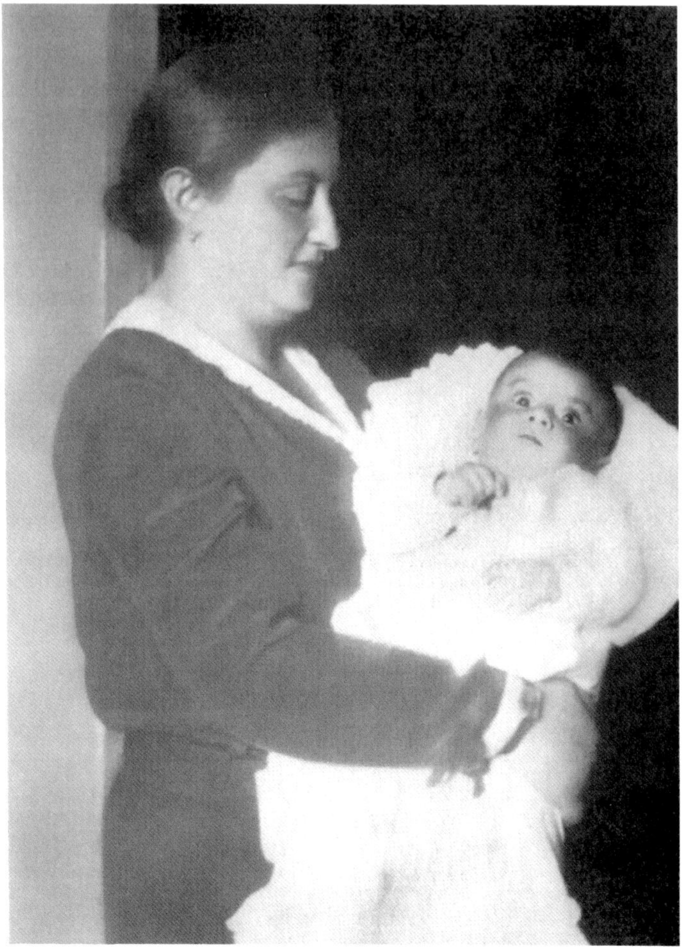

Pictured is Frieda Garfunkel and her baby, Felix, in 1929. Felix survived three years at the Moghilev concentration camp in the Ukraine. *Courtesy of Felix Garfunkel.*

family in the town of North Hamptonshire, England. The family took very good care of him and treated him like a son. Weil was unable to move out of England during the war. He did not know of the Holocaust until after the war, when he was able to travel to New York City and move in with his aunt in 1945. One year later, he was drafted into the army. He was at first stationed in postwar Germany in 1946. Through the army, Weil was able to take advantage of the new GI Bill, which allowed him to go back to school. For each month served, the government paid for a certain amount of college tuition, plus an additional year of free schooling. By the time he graduated high school, Weil had enough money to pay for college and selected Kent State University in Kent, Ohio. There, he stayed with a close friend of his New York cousin and earned a bachelor of science degree in accounting in 1950.

"It was very emotional returning to Germany," Weil said. He was apprehensive to go back, knowing what had happened to his family and his people. Postwar Germany had been divided up into four sectors, with eastern Germany then communist.

Weil's career began in Dayton, Ohio, in 1950, and five years later, he met his wife, Frances, a Canadian, while traveling through the Adirondacks to Lake Placid. It was love at first sight, he said. They begin courting as he drove the nine hundred miles to visit her until they were married in 1955. He stayed with Arthur Beerman's meatpacking plant from 1955 until its closure in 1968. From there, Weil spent the next five years with another Dayton retailer, Liberal Markets grocery chain. Five years later, Liberal Markets closed, and Weil and his wife went together into the commercial art business in 1973, forming a commercial gallery called Enterprise Gallerie. Weil and his family sold high-priced paintings and lithographs to law offices and hospitals. Many of these works of art sold for $500 to $600 each. They sold art at art shows and auctions and traveled together throughout the Midwest Ohio, Indiana, Pennsylvania and Michigan. They stayed in business for twenty-two years, from 1973 to 1995. Their inventory included works by Norman Rockwell, Salvadore Dali and others.

The art business changed again in the mid-1990s, when many commercial studios went out of business. Weil decided it was time to retire. Widowed now with two children and four grandchildren, Weil hasn't slowed down yet. Today, he teaches adult learning courses on the Holocaust, called the "Rise and Fall of the Third Reich," not to be confused with the book of the same name. There, Weil talks about the Holocaust, his personal experiences of survival and the period of history when it was a death sentence to be Jewish. He volunteers periodically at the National Museum of the United States Air Force.

"The most important thing for people to understand is that hatred leads to oppression and misunderstanding between people," Weil said. "The early anti-Semitism that kept Jewish children out of the U.S. during their most desperate hour would be unthinkable today, but the rising ethnic hatred in Europe has bandied now more than ever since the end of World War II. America is ideal in terms of peace. We have peaceful neighbors to the north (Canada) and to the south (Mexico) and Latin America. We are also separated from the world's skirmishes by two vast oceans: the Pacific and the Atlantic."

Felix Garfunkel

Felix Garfunkel was in a concentration camp from age ten to thirteen; he was emaciated and overcome with different diseases like typhus and abscesses due to malnutrition and the threat of being killed anytime. It was by the Soviet forces winning and advancing west, pushing the Nazi troops back, that Garfunkel and his compatriots were liberated.

"We walked back home in a period of several weeks," he said.

Garfunkel lived in the concentration camps for three years. His family had suffered terrible persecutions and starvation. "I have succeeded and studied and made a good career. I have a wife and children: a son who is an anesthesiologist." His daughter, now deceased, was a rabbi. Dr. Garfunkel came to Dayton to work at Greene Memorial Hospital early in 1965 and worked as the director of radiology and nuclear medicine until 1992. Garfunkel and his family stayed in Dayton and Cincinnati because the people were friendly and it was easy to get around.

Garfunkel belongs to Temple Israel on North Main Street in Dayton. He was given an honorary position as speaker chair of political science at Wright State University and was called on many times to explain the turmoil in Europe at the time of Nazi occupation. Garfunkel spoke to medical students and to University of Dayton students studying the Holocaust. He said:

> *There is still much anti-Semitism and ethnic tension in Europe. I am very concerned about the plight of the Jews in France and Belgium. Human beings are always fighting wars. If you look at history, we are very fortunate to be in this wonderful best country in the world and protected by our citizenship.*
>
> *If you go to Russia today, there everybody is not equal. Unfortunately every dictator thinks that he is justified in killing people. See with* [the Islamic states of Iraq and Syria], *I think they are doing something to help their cause—doing something for the people. The problem is we all have different interpretations of peace…There is not anyone anywhere that is not affected by the cruelty to all of life.*

Often the reason for the anti-Semitism is very simple. Garfunkel continued:

> *They know anti-Semitism with no education on what's going on in the Middle East. People here in the U.S. understand we will never have another Holocaust and we will wipe out bigotry and hatred. In Europe and the Middle East, people are ignorant as to what a Jew is.*

Germany today, however, is different, as the county has built quite a few memorials to the Holocaust. However, in Belgium thousands are moving to Israel. [Seven] *percent of France is Muslim. The French Muslims are taught hatred because they believe that Jews are oppressing the Palestinians. In France they read the bias in the papers, which are published with a Muslim perspective. Important to know is that even though these atrocities did not take place here, Dayton has made cultural education a higher priority.*

Denmark did not permit the Nazis to take the Jews. Bulgaria was not allowed to take Romanian Jews. We in the periphery, as the Nazis said, were communist and sent to concentration camp. Seven hundred thousand Jews were killed in Romania and Transylvania. In Moldavia, they took 350,000. Hungary would not permit the Nazis to take the Jews from there in 1944 so they went to Hungary and forcibly took the Jews. That is how [Holocaust survivor] *Elie Weisel was taken.*

Nobody was prepared. England and the U.S. were not prepared. It was a terrible war—30 million people died in this war. The Nazis were allowed to invade who they wanted—they were the strongest military power in Europe until they were defeated in Stalingrad by the Soviet army.

Somehow our species cannot seem to hold still. But, whoever works for peace makes a difference.

4

CIVIC ENGAGEMENT

ACCOUNTABILITY AND PRESERVATION

From 1850 to 1890, the Native American population in the continental United States shriveled from 400,000 down to 248,000. Years later, environmental conservation, including the establishment of the Miami Conservancy District during the 1913 flood relief, brought a resurgence of native artifacts that the native cultures left behind. Ecology became a major concern in the late twentieth century, beginning with the reclamation of the Miami Valley's water supply.

Eleven sites relating to Dayton aviation heritage were restored and recovered. Some museums were created in Dayton to celebrate the history and continuing education of areas of local and national significance. Included in those sites are the National Museum of the United States Air Force and the Armstrong Air and Space Museum. The EPA mandated major cleanup to help preserve the Dayton region's water supply and topsoil from corrosion and pollution.

National Cash Register and the Flood Cleanup, 1913

Throughout the late nineteenth and early twentieth centuries, NCR enjoyed an almost legendary reputation. Several notable NCR employees and associates made a lasting impact on the improvement of the human

Machinists work in full production at NCR in 1902. *Courtesy of the Detroit Publishing Company.*

condition. In 1879, a saloonkeeper in Dayton named John Ritty thought his employees were stealing. About the same time, he went on a voyage to Europe and toured the ship's engine room. Fascinated by the indicator that recorded the rotations of the propeller shaft, Ritty adapted what he had seen in the engine room to a cabinet with keys in rows of five-cent increments, creating the first cash register. This tabulated the day's sales, which could be compared with the cash receipts collected. Soon after, John H. Patterson bought Ritty's invention for $6,500 and started up the National Manufacturing Company. In 1884, Patterson changed the name of his company to form the National Cash Register (NCR) into one of the first modern American companies. The first sales training school in the nation was established at NCR in 1893. NCR's training school guaranteed territories and sales training course manuals. Patterson also introduced a comprehensive social welfare program for his factory workers and sales force.

John H. Patterson's employee welfare programs at NCR were imitated throughout the country. In the early twentieth century, NCR was the largest employer in Dayton, with the best pay and most benefits to offer. After 1897, Patterson was known to have paid his employees for ten hours' work on a nine-

Great Miami flood survivors signal rescuers from the top of the NCR Building, 1913. *Courtesy of Bain News Service.*

and-half-hour day. In 1917, Patterson instituted a profit-sharing program and an employee welfare program. Employees without plumbing or running water at home could shower at work. Employees were encouraged to engage in the no-cost, company-sponsored social events, including horseback riding and golf.

NCR stayed progressive through the Depression: one-sixth of all American corporate executives were trained at NCR between the years 1910 and 1930. Despite the value placed on his employees, Patterson's reputation as a ruthless, erudite businessman still exceeded him until the panic caused by the great flood of 1913.

During the Great Miami flood of 1913, which made national headlines, 10,000 persons were displaced. In the storm, 360 people died in Dayton and surrounding areas. Overall, there were 700 casualties throughout the state of Ohio. Thousands of livestock were killed. The town of Osborn, near present-day Fairborn, was literally ripped from its location due to flood damage.

When floodwaters struck the community, a few refugees fled to St. Mary's College, which was built high on a hill south of downtown Dayton, incorporated as the University of Dayton in 1920. The college was uniquely

The north side of Ludlow Street was completely submerged during the Great Miami flood of 1913. *Courtesy of Bain News Service.*

situated and equipped to provide relief to flood victims. The first night, four hundred refugees took shelter at St. Mary's College; by the end of the week, the number had grown to six hundred. In all, the college assisted eight hundred refugees.

Because the students had not returned from Easter break, the college kitchen was stocked with food and provisions. Due to its location on the hill, electric light and heating plants were not affected, a plentiful clean water supply was available and the college had other essential facilities such as a laundry and infirmary. The college's kitchen provided meals to Miami Valley Hospital and twelve thousand pounds of provisions to St. Elizabeth Hospital.

Once the flood survivors had been rescued, flood relief and cleanup were underway. Patterson and the city commission struggled to raise money and find a suitable engineer to restore the community and prevent the problem of future flooding. Patterson had taken it upon himself to recruit the finest hydraulic engineer in the country, civil engineer Arthur E. Morgan, to cleanup. Within five days of the flood, Patterson held a private rally at Sugarcamp, NCR's training campus, to encourage business owners and private citizens to cooperate and donate supplies and relief funds for the flood cleanup.

Rescue workers during the Great Miami flood of 1913 volunteer emergency first response. *Courtesy of Bain News Service.*

The city proper raised $2,212,000 in two months to hire Morgan and to construct a flood-control system in the Miami Valley. Patterson pledged to match donations from the NCR pep rally to repair the city. Combined, the company and matched donations raised $500,000, the equivalent of about $10 million today. Morgan was tasked to build five dry reservoirs in the Greater Dayton area, which would control water flow and institute a recanalization to relieve rising water levels and prevent a future flood. This was known as the hydraulic jump method.

Dayton was the first large American city to adopt the city-manager form of municipal government after the flood of 1913. These plans were instituted in the Miami Valley through the Miami Conservancy District, between 1913 and about 1921. By 1980, 2,500 other American cities had adopted a similar city-commissioned management system.

Morgan's solution was a proposed system of dry, earthen dams to control the river systems above Dayton. To the north is the Loramie River, near Piqua. To the south is Twin Creek, near Germantown. Mad River is near Fairborn, and Stillwater is near Englewood. The Great Miami flows out near Vandalia. In 1914, the State of Ohio passed the Conservancy Act, which authorized stream drainage areas to form flood-control agencies. On June 28, 1915, the Miami Conservancy District was created and headquartered in Dayton. The work on the Miami Conservancy District, of which the Huffman Dam was the first built, required twenty-one draglines, twenty-nine locomotives and two hundred dump cars. Because of the sustainability of flood prevention implemented in Dayton in 1913, Morgan was chosen in 1933 by President Franklin Delano Roosevelt to design and deploy the Tennessee Valley system of dams for flood control and electrification. Morgan, socially conscientious and intent on reform, joined the Quakers and became a member of the Yellow Springs' Society of Friends.

Morgan became a member of the board of trustees of Antioch College in Yellow Springs in 1919. In 1920, he was appointed president of Antioch, a position he held until 1936. As president, Morgan stressed the need for students to become well-rounded human beings, focusing on making a contribution rather than just concentrating on a field of study. Under his leadership, the college gained a national reputation for its quality education. Morgan introduced an innovative concept that he called "work-study" during his time as Antioch's president. Students attended classes for one term and then took time off to work as interns in the outside world.

Antioch College was built in 1853 in Yellow Springs by A.M. Merrifield. *Courtesy of A.M. Merrifield and the Historic American Buildings Survey.*

Among other accomplishments in the 1940s, he founded a nonprofit organization to promote small communities (the Community Service, Inc.), which helped set up a system of rural universities in India and fought to protect Native American (the Senecas) land from flooding. The U.S. Army Corps of Engineers set up this program.

Preserving Dayton Native Lands

The Dayton Project was an official site of the Manhattan Project—where the United States built the atom bomb. Monsanto, the chemical and food additive giant, took over the book repository for the City of Dayton over on West First Street, which had been built in the latter part of the 1890s. The reason for this acquisition was to maintain creative control over Monsanto research scientist Charles Allen Thomas, who was recruited by the Manhattan Project to coordinate plutonium purification. To accomplish this work in Dayton, Monsanto took over Bonebrake Seminary, located on First Street and Euclid Avenue. After that, a new laboratory was built out in Northwest Dayton. A third site for the Dayton Project was built in 1943, just southwest of Dayton, near an ancient Indian burial site on Mound Road.

Indian Mound Hill

The indigenous peoples of North America did not believe in owning the land—they wanted only to preserve it. The Mound Builders of Ohio, formerly Adena and Hopewell tribes, built a mound effigy in Miamisburg, Ohio, located south of Dayton, which dates back an estimated two thousand to three thousand years ago. First uncovered in 1869, it is one of about one thousand effigy mounds remaining in Ohio. Effigy mounds are the earthen constructions discovered in the shape of animals, birds, trees and the famous Serpent Mound of Warren County. An estimated one-tenth of the earthen burial mounds of Ohio mounds have survived.

Standing sixty-seven feet high and eight hundred feet in circumference, the Serpent Mound is the second-largest Indian burial mound east of the Mississippi River. Layers of dirt piled upward on top of one another revealed a different burial with each layer. Today, the site is 90 percent undisturbed and remains a refuge and park reserve for the residents of the city of Miamisburg and their families to enjoy during warmer weather.

Within a mile of this ancient Adena historical site, Monsanto's facility was built to continue the polonium-related work being done at the Dayton Project units. Located at the southern edge of Miamisburg, fifteen miles due south of Dayton, Mound Laboratory became operational in 1949 and was the United States' first postwar Atomic Energy Commission site to be constructed.

Scientists at Mound Laboratories continued to research and manufacture polonium-based initiators for nuclear weapons throughout the Cold War, as was the basis for the Dayton Project work in World War II. Their research also included exploring alternate fuels for the initiator since polonium-210's relatively short half-life meant that the initiator would need to be replaced every five months. At Mound, two elements were introduced: actinium-227 and polonium-208, both of which have longer half-lives. A half-life is the amount of time required for a quantity of radiation to fall to half its value. The project was codenamed "Urchin" and conducted in secrecy.

Once considered the largest employer of Miamisburg residents, 1,706 individuals were employed by the Monsanto Corporation during the Cold War. Beginning in 1960, the Mound released radioactive tritium into the air and contaminated the soil with plutonium-238. Miamisburg's city water supply was piped up Indian Mound Hill, the site of the ancient earthen Indian mound. Children played up at the Adena Indian mound and swam in the community swimming pool built adjacent to it. The Department of Energy (DOE) regulated Mound Plant, which was was operated by Monsanto from its opening until 1988. The primary mission of the Mound Plant was the development, engineering, manufacturing and evaluation of explosive components for the United States' nuclear defense stockpile. The Mound Plant was placed on the DOE's National Priorities List in 1989 due to past waste disposal practices and releases to the environment. As a result, cleanup efforts were initiated under the Comprehensive Environmental Response, Compensation and Liabilities Act (CERCLA, also known as Superfund).

Out of concern for the people living in the area, the DOE interviewed around two hundred residents over a three-and-a-half-year period. Residents in and around Miamisburg were given the opportunity to express concerns over radioactive and nonradioactive (hazardous) substances originating from the Mound Plant. Some residents claim that they and their families suffered more than average occurrences of cancer within the radioactive treatment area of Mound Laboratories.

Popular opinion was that the environment might have contained traces of harmful radiation. The DOE continues to run yearly samplings on air, ground water, surface water, sediment, fish, vegetation and produce for potential off-site contamination. In addition, on-site sampling of soil, surface water, air and ground water was conducted to monitor cleanup investigations and to clean up under a cost recovery grant.

In response to pressing concerns of the residents of Miamisburg surveyed, the DOE issued a statement:

> *When all response and remedial actions have been performed within a release block, it is necessary to evaluate risks to human health due to any residual contamination that may remain in the given release block. A risk evaluation is performed to determine that future industrial/commercial use of the land will not subject users to unacceptable health risks. The evaluation is performed prior to transfer of the release block.*[13]

In Dayton, in 1994, all production and research at Mound Laboratories, with the exception of the Space Nuclear Auxiliary Power (SNAP) generator program, stopped. The SNAP program officially ceased, and cleanup of the site began the following year. The Mound Science and Energy Museum was later established to preserve the remaining heritage of the Mound Laboratory, its workers and its site. The Ohio Environmental Protection Agency (EPA) prepared an annual report to disclose to the public that documented environmental oversight activities at the Mound Plant. The report provides interested parties a source of information regarding the state's regulatory, environmental monitoring, public outreach and planning activities for three consecutive years, beginning in 1995.

Today, the EPA has a better understanding of the potentially hazardous and permanently damaging effects of radiation and toxic chemicals to plant and animal life. The Ohio EPA and the Dayton-area Superfund grant, begun in 1989, have continued to improve living conditions of wildlife and green growth in the Miami Valley. With this thorough collection of data and environmental testing, the EPA insists the site is safe for all living creatures and free from harmful levels of radiation.

Inside the Mound Cleanup Project

Systems engineer Doug Keener left Mound Laboratories in 1992. Keener is now one of 4,600 permanent employees at the Oak Ridge, Tennessee nuclear test site, Oak Ridge National Laboratories, or ORNL. At ORNL, he is in charge of testing and systems checks. Oak Ridge was the original site of the plutonium production used in the Manhattan Project to build the bomb Little Boy. No nuclear weapons have been built since the Cold War, but billions of dollars are spent every year—on this and three other key nationally licensed nuclear test centers and building sites—to maintain the safety and operability of the mass store of nuclear arms.

Keener worked on the first cleanup project, which began in the mid-'80s. The Cold War was ending, and Keener left the plant just shortly after. He was not involved in the Mound 2000 effort of 1996–97, in which the second of two buildings was closed permanently. The mission had ended for that particular facility, and there were legacy issues left over from the work that

The Department of Energy, Building B, Mound Facility, on One Mound Road, was built in 1947. *Courtesy of U.S. Atomic Energy Commission.*

was conducted there. Part of the original plant built for the Dayton Project would have to be torn down. The DOE closed the loop on the Manhattan Project in Dayton.

Keener said, "There were a number of buildings out there at the time. The other processing facility was still being used in a limited fashion for research. They had redirected their efforts for moving." Keener is a degreed mechanical engineer who graduated from Purdue University in 1989. Hired by Mound Laboratories as a decommissioning engineer, this was Keener's first job out of college. His role involved the surgical deconstruction of the building of the facility used to process radioactive materials.

"The legacy contamination issues inside required us to implement controls to ensure the decom was captured and disposed of as you go," he said. "We had to demolish the building from the inside out. Afterward, they removed external decontamination from the internal structure decom. Also, my role was to establish the technical methods for removing waste from the building."

Keener was not prepared for this role while studying at Purdue, but he had some pre-employment training authorized by the DOE before the start of the project. He was a new grad working on a new venture with the government.

"This was a new job, and the first cleanup effort in the area. We were expected to gain on-the-job experience." However, during his tenure, he was fully confident that he and the rest of the crew were not going in there blind. His supervisors had historical knowledge of the facility and what kind of work had occurred before and after the dropping of the bomb.

Radiological surveys had been conducted prior to the cleanup project. "They found things that didn't quite make sense," Keener said. "That's what you get when a building is used over years' and years' time. Not all the history is going to be complete. We had general understanding of the ventilation systems. It was easy to anticipate that the highest levels of contamination were going to be captured, and we had to adjust strategies to be able to handle that."

The primary safety precaution was respiratory protection. Mandatory respiratory gear protected and covered all areas of skin on the body—coveralls, shoe coverings and rubber gloves, very similar to HAZMAT gear. Keener required continuous wear of the protective gear.

"The objective was to try and get natural levels of background radiation stabilized." Radiation, he said, exists everywhere in the natural world. "There is no such thing as zero radiation," he said. "The only option is to remove whatever had been added through the processing."

The result was that they saw a reduction in radiation levels, and progress was measurable. As to how the radioactive materials were broken down, the process involved packaging shipments to a disposal facility, most often in Nevada. Even the building itself was packaged and shipped to the test lab in Nevada for disposal. Once decommissioned, the soil from the lab area is considered safe for planting. The former site is adjacent to the Indian burial mound. No radiation leaks were detected there during the cleanup effort. Keener's objective to safely package the contamination and deconstruct the materials in the first of the two buildings was accomplished successfully within the time estimated. Keener has thought quite a lot about why Mound Laboratories was built in the first place. Keener said:

> *What we understood was in hindsight: People at the time didn't know what they were dealing with: capabilities of the atom had not been understood. Unfortunate, too, was that so much secrecy went on. At the time, we were at war, and dropping the bomb was determined as necessary for the end goal of winning the war. It was unfortunate in the events that followed that so many people got hurt directly as a result of misunderstanding of what they were dealing with—not malicious intent to put people in harm's way. What we know today regarding the generational impact of the bombings in Japan and how the effects are much more understood have led to a greater awareness of the effects of radiation exposure. We are benefitting from the sacrifices made from individuals in the past. All are smarter for it…just unfortunate some accidents did happen. In hindsight, we believed the war had to be stopped. The thinking was about the Japanese people as a proud nation and they were not going to surrender.*
>
> *In the book* Unbroken*—it was the history of what happened to the Japanese people at the time. They were decimated economically, and the people were starving. The Emperor was not going to give up and was determined to fight to the last man. What they saw then was the overwhelming force from the atom bomb.*
>
> *Today, we just want the right people in charge of that threat of force; we hope that we have the right people in charge of the "switch."*

Keener and his family moved out to Tennessee in the mid-'90s to perform more decommissioning work for the ORNL. In 1999, he switched industries to work for a company that did projects for the Tennessee Valley Authority (TVA). He later ended up back in Oak Ridge. Part of his job now is to keep the ORNL facility operating and to keep the public safe.

After twenty years in the business, Keener said he had incurred no long-term health crises as a result of working either at Mound Laboratories or the ORNL.

"As long as you respect nuclear energy and follow prescribed methods for dealing with it, it can be handled safely," he said.

With the continuous advent of Occupational Safety and Health Administration safety regulations, many of the early nightmares in nuclear research can now be avoided, as the DOE endeavors to explore uses for nuclear energy in a safe and efficient manner.

The Discovery of an Ancient Village

On Nicholas Road, near the University of Dayton, a twentieth-century discovery was made through an EPA-mandated cleanup project and excavated under the Wastewater Treatment Act of 1987.

The wastewater treatment plant (WWTP) is located at its original 1929 site in the southwest corner of the city of Dayton, on the Great Miami River. At this point on the river, the wastewater discharged from the WWTP can contribute up to 40 to 50 percent of the total river flow during low-flow (drought) conditions. This large contribution to river flow requires the wastewater discharged to meet the cleanest water-quality standards to protect warm water aquatic animals and plants, as well as to allow for other designated uses like fishing, boating and skiing. The Wastewater Treatment Act of 1987 required a higher degree of filtration and treatment than with the previous Clean Water Act. The WWTP was told not to expand into the Indian village historical site, as it was still under excavation. Standards for clean water were expected to be higher going forward. It was not until late in the next year, 1988, that excavation on the Indian Village archaeological site was completed. Until then, excavators were told to go around it.

Dayton Society for Natural History archaeologist William Kennedy said the Indian village—now known as the local historical site, museum and tourist attraction SunWatch Indian Village—was discovered by farmers on the Vance farm. The WWTP belongs to the city of Dayton and, in the 1960s, had decided to take on a new function treating sludge ponds adjacent to the water treatment facility. As farmers began digging, Kennedy said, they discovered human remains, and as the excavation began to open up, it became apparent that this was a find of historical significance.

SunWatch, as it was named, was built around AD 1200 in a pattern of concentric circles with burial plots, trash pits and storage bins fanning out from the central plane. The Fort Ancient people tended to build robust villages populated with around 100 to 500 residents; SunWatch was populated by an estimated 250 people. This number varied with the season, as people would leave the village in the winter to live in hunting camps. The villages were substantially larger and more sedentary than the Late Woodland tribes and were occupied for at least twenty to thirty years.

This was no ordinary find. Some earthen works sites in Southwest Ohio date back to 9000 BC—the ice age. The Dayton Society for Natural History owns and operates the SunWatch Indian Village and the Boonshoft Museum of Discovery. Operated as an open-air museum, the three-acre site is preserved as a national site of historical significance.

Dayton's Most Celebrated Museums

Dayton, Ohio's National Museum of the Air Force located on the Wright-Patterson Air Force Base is the oldest aviation museum in the world. The museum was started to trace America's entire legacy of flight and retell its peace resolution efforts from the early years of the Wright brothers through World War II and the Cold War. Exhibits on the space age technology and twenty-first-century conflicts in the Middle East are on display at the museum to commemorate both the sacrifice and courage of those who explored new worlds or died courageously in battle.

Engineers from Dayton's McCook Field first began collecting artifacts in 1923. The artifact recovery operation moved to a laboratory in Wright Field in 1927. Then in 1932, the collection was named the Army Aeronautical Museum and placed in a Works Progress Administration building from 1935 until after World War II. In 1948, this private collection was called the Air Force Technical Museum. In 1954, the Air Force Museum went public and opened its first permanent building, Building 89, an entire hanger of the former Patterson Field in Fairborn. The museum kept retired aircraft parked outside and remained there until 1971, when the current iteration opened. Since 1971, the museum has tripled in square footage.

The museum changed its name in October 2004 from the United States Air Force Museum to the National Museum of the United States Air Force. Many military planes, whether or not they were actually manufactured

Above: The WPAFB radio aircraft test lab, from McCook Field, was used as a testing field and for aviation experiments starting in 1917. *Courtesy of the Historic American Buildings Survey.*

Right: Experiments in the Vertical Wind Tunnel Lab at WPAFB began after the creation of the base in 1948. *Courtesy of the Historic American Buildings Survey.*

Left: An exterior shot of Vertical Wind Tunnel Lab at WPAFB. Historic buildings were transferred to Wright Field in 1927. *Courtesy of the Historic American Buildings Survey.*

Below: The WPAFB, area B, Signal Corps Special Forces hangar was transferred from Wright Field in 1948. *Historic American Engineering Record.*

The WPAFB eighty-four-inch test dynamometer was part of the area B buildings, number 31, the aircraft assembly hangar. *Courtesy of the Historic American Buildings Survey.*

in Southwest Ohio, are permanently displayed in the museum. A fourth building, added in 2015, houses the Space Gallery, the Presidential Aircraft Gallery and the Global Reach Gallery. There, visitors can see the Crew Compartment Trainer One, CCT-1, which was used to teach astronauts how to fly orbiters and operate equipment in space. A full-scale mock-up of the payload bay was created as part of the exhibit.

Man on the Moon

On July 16, 1969, a thirty-six-story rocket blasted off from Cape Kennedy, Florida, in what would be the emancipation of man from the bonds of the Earth. During Neil Armstrong's last interview in 2012, he recounted the crew's death-defying twelve-minute descent to the moon. The computer charted the shuttle's landing in an unstable location. Before lift-off, it was

This photo of the moonwalk was taken from the shuttle of the Apollo 11 on July 20, 1969. *Courtesy of NASA archives.*

estimated that the crew of Apollo 11 sustained a fifty-fifty chance of survival in landing on the lunar surface.

On July 20, 1969, at 4:18 p.m., Armstrong, using his fighter pilot skills, navigated the lunar module crew of the Apollo 11 to a safe touchdown, with less than twenty seconds of fuel remaining in the shuttle, at Tranquility Base, located in the Sea of Tranquility. The region was so named because it appeared to astronomers in the 1600s to be an actual body of water. Referring to the lunar module, the Eagle, Armstrong reported, "The Eagle has landed." At 10:56 p.m., Armstrong descended from the Eagle's ladder, touched one foot to the moon's surface and announced, "That's one small step for man, one giant leap for mankind." Armstrong's famous faux pas, in which he delivered the line without the word "a" in the sentence, was a result of nerves.

This is the gold replica of an olive branch, the traditional symbol of peace, left on the moon's surface by Apollo 11 crewmembers. *Courtesy of NASA archives.*

Edwin "Buzz" Aldrin soon joined Armstrong for a walk on this stark, strange landscape, collecting soil and rock samples. Aldrin set up the American flag. Moon dust has its own unique smell and properties, according to the moon-landing astronauts. Its texture is very clingy and smells of discharged gunpowder.

Twenty-four astronauts were born in Ohio. Eight are from Cleveland; one is from Dayton; one from Troy, just north of Dayton; and Neil Armstrong is from Wapakoneta, forty-eight miles north of Dayton. Charles Bassett was the astronaut from Dayton, and Nancy Curry was the one from Troy. Armstrong's hometown of Wapakoneta was established by Shawnee Indians and literally means "white-cloth" to demonstrate neutrality with the Indians after the signing of the Treaty of Greenville.

Armstrong was an Ohio boy at heart and notoriously stayed away from the limelight. He retired from NASA in 1971 and became a University of Cincinnati professor of engineering for ten years. He bought a two-hundred-acre dairy farm in Lebanon, Ohio, between Dayton and Cincinnati. Armstrong earned a bachelor's degree in aeronautical engineering from Purdue University in 1955. In 1970, he earned a master's degree in aerospace engineering from the University of Southern California. Armstrong had flown seventy-eight combat missions in Korea. He was a daring test pilot who soared in the X-15. Armstrong passed away on August 24, 2012.

Armstrong's legendary life can be revisited in the Neil Armstrong Space Museum in Wapakoneta. The museum houses the Gemini VIII spacecraft, Neil Armstrong's Gemini and Apollo spacesuits and an Apollo 11 moon rock. The museum is also home to two full-sized aircraft, both of which were flown by Armstrong during the Korean War. Visitors can practice landing the lunar module and space shuttle and recount the dramatic events of the historic lunar landing.

5

THE BALKAN PROXIMITY PEACE TALKS

Dayton Model for Peace

The Wright-Patterson Air Force Base, the Eighty-eight Wing Command, was among the first wing commands built at the inception of the air force in 1947. This agency was instituted, at first, to prepare flight equipment and pilots for war and international conflict resolution and to provide safety and security for civilians and military personnel.

As society neared the twenty-first century, another first for Dayton and the world took place at the Wright-Patterson Air Force Base. Without a single shot fired, delegates from three warring factions in Bosnia met and sequestered in separate quarters at the base to draw up a peace agreement to end the war in Bosnia. This process became known in diplomatic circles as the Dayton model for peace, or a "Dayton."

In October 1995, Secretary of State Warren M. Christopher and then assistant secretary of state for European and Canadian affairs Richard C. Holbrooke presented the besieged nation of Bosnia and Herzegovina with an ultimatum.

The North American Treaty Organization (NATO) promised a ceasefire of the bombing against the Bosnian Serbs, who committed 90 percent of the atrocities in the war in Bosnia, if the country's leaders would agree to travel to a host summit in Dayton, Ohio. Should they refuse, the United States, sanctioned by the UN, would continue with NATO bombings and send in American ground troop support to break the Serbian stronghold in Bosnia.

President Slobodan Milošević of the Socialist Federal Republic of Yugoslavia, President Franjo Tuđman of Croatia and President Alija Izetbegović of Bosnia and Herzegovina (with his foreign minister, Muhamed Sacirbey) agreed to talk peace. The presidents and ministers of these countries would meet to create the General Framework Agreement for Peace in Dayton at the Wright-Patterson Air Force Base. The bid for peace, called a "Dayton" by those in the diplomatic community, was the first of its kind in the world and became a template for the modern era to resolve conflict without bloodshed.

A Country Torn Apart

After the defeat of the Turks on Kosovo Field in the year 1389, three distinct religious groups took over to live harmoniously together for centuries in the Balkans of Europe: the Christian Orthodox Serbs, the Catholic Croatians and the Muslims (Bosniaks).

Ambassador Holbrooke wrote:

> *One of my most vivid memories from my trip to Yugoslavia in 1960 was the beautiful sixteenth-century bridge linking the two parts of Mostar. It was perhaps Yugoslavia's most famous symbol of multiethnic harmony. When I last saw the high-arched bridge in 1992, it was crumbling by continuous shelling by the Croats, pathetically protected by automobile tires hung over the sides on ropes. Two years later, in September 1994, when I visited Mostar with General Charles Boyd, the Deputy Commander in Chief of U.S. Forces in Europe, the bridge was gone, replaced by a narrow, swaying metal footbridge hundreds of feet above the Neretva River which Boyd and I cautiously crossed, stepping over gaping holes in the steel planking.*[14]

During the Cold War, the Socialist Federal Republic of Yugoslavia was ruled by communist autocrat Marshal Josip Broz Tito from 1943 to 1980.

Opposite, top: WPAFB, area B, building number 31, was among the historic property transferred to Wright Field beginning in 1927. *Courtesy of Courtesy of the Historic American Buildings Survey.*

Opposite, bottom: The Supersonic Test Laboratory in Building 26 was part of the McCook Field complex built in 1917. *Courtesy of the Historic American Buildings Survey.*

Within ten years after Tito's death, with only a facile conflict resolution to settle territory disputes, the country of Yugoslavia was torn apart. No one had the same magnetism to unify the territory after Tito. Instead, each of the three groups conspired to gain control of the republic without a common goal or interest.

In February 29, 1992, Bosnia and Herzegovina (BiH) managed to proclaim independence. However, Bosnian Serbs rebelled through the leadership of Radovan Karadzic and created their own separate state in Bosnia—the Serb Republic or Republika Srpska (RS). They did not want to recognize Macedonia or acknowledge the Nation of Islam as Tito had.

Radio Television Belgrade, broadcast under Slobodan Milošević's and Franjo Tuđman's approval, sensationalized an institutional nationalism against the Bosniaks, or the Bosnian Muslims, from 1991 to '92. An entire generation of Serbs, Croats and Muslims—suffering from poverty, dissolution and joblessness—were aroused by television to again hate their neighbors.[15] American journalists had photographed some of the atrocities being committed against the Bosniaks in the Serbs' prison camps that went ignored at first by the Western world. Several wars broke out in the Balkans in the decade between 1991 and 2001, including the Yugoslav invasion of Slovenia, the Croats and Serbs, the Serbs and the Bosnians and the Croats and Bosnians.

Before the Dayton agreement in 1995, the Bosnian Serbs controlled about 46 percent of the land in BiH; Bosniaks controlled 28 percent; and Bosnian Croats had about 25 percent. However, Muslims made up the majority, 44 percent, of the population; the Serbs were 32 percent of the population; and the Croats ranked third, with 17 percent.

Unopposed by the United Nations Protection Force (UNPROFOR), the Bosnian Serbs controlled the army and got behind the RS power base. The RS seized part of Croatia and 70 percent of Bosnia and lashed out to kill or expel Muslims from the region. At the same time, the Croatian army helped Croats in Bosnia take over much of the western portion of Herzegovina to claim Mostar, not Sarajevo, as its capital.

This policy of ethnic cleansing resulted in a wave of Muslim refugees pouring into other countries. Muslim refugees spilled into Germany by the thousands, but Europe and America stayed out of the conflict. The Muslims were left with no land or citizenship and began a fight for survival.

An emergency Washington agreement was drafted in 1994 to impose a federation, but this did not hold. Bosnia had committed 90 percent of all the atrocities in the Bosnian war and went unchallenged, obliterating the designated UN safe areas. The RS had turned BiH into a bloodbath.

Favored by the Yugoslav People's Army with a brutal military superiority, the RS was given most of the artillery and armaments from the former communist nation to further its bloody campaign.

The world was watching and could no longer ignore the crimes against humanity, such as the shelling of the Sarajevo marketplace on February 5, 1994; the May 1995 seizure of UN peace-keepers to use as human shields; or the infamous July 1995 massacre of eight thousand Muslim men and boys who were rounded up, tortured and killed in a Srebrenica soccer field. All of these events were broadcast around the world via CNN.

UN countries called the massacre at Srebrenica the worst single act against humanity in Europe since World War II. The killing was ordered under General Ratko Mladic and instrumented, in part, by a Serbian paramilitary group, called the Scorpions, as well as a few hundred Ukrainian and Russian volunteers. The surviving women and girls from the Srebrenica massacre were raped.

The UN began bombing Serbian installations from the air without sending in ground troops to try to put pressure on the Bosnian Serbs to stop the combat hail of artillery against the Croatians and the gross massacre of the Muslims. The city of Sarajevo was left without heat or electricity. Many of the hotels and apartment buildings inhabited by survivors and refugees were just bombed-out shells.

The Clinton administration finally decided to take the initiative and send veteran diplomat Richard Holbrooke to lead an all-out negotiating effort to end the war in Bosnia. Holbrooke and his team would mediate between the three sides—the Federal Republish of Yugoslavia (FRY), Croatia and BiH to reverse what had been characterized as the "greatest collective failure of the West since the 1930s."

Mission for Peace

In August, one month after the Srebrenica massacre, Robert Frasure, Joseph Kruzel and Colonel Sam Nelson Drew—three of Holbrooke's most trusted colleagues from the Vietnam era—set out for Sarajevo to pursue hardline negotiations to stem the bloodletting. These were some of the most seasoned diplomats in the field.

If the meetings proved unsuccessful, America would be drawn into a war that the people would not support. Holbrooke and his colleagues knew from cumulative diplomatic experiences during the Vietnam era that American people would not get behind a military action in Bosnia. The loss of American life would be substantial in a three-sided conflict.

Former secretary of state Colin Powell echoed the sentiment in his memoirs:

> *Many of my generation: the career Captains, the Majors and Lieutenants, and Colonels seasoned in that* [Vietnam] *war, vowed that when our turn came to call the shots, we would not quietly acquiesce in half-hearted warfare for half-baked reasons that the American people could not understand or support.*[16]

Still, they had to do something.

To reach the Bosnian capital of Sarajevo, the trio was to travel over the most dangerous route in Europe: the Mount Igman road. Although the Serbs agreed to a cease-fire to allow the convoy through, the mission was compromised. The mountain roads were more dangerous to travel, but the group could not risk going through the main roads, which were overrun by Serb checkpoints. On the day they were scheduled to arrive on the Mount Igman road, August 19, 1995, the first vehicle, carrying Frasure, Kruzel and Drew, suddenly slid down the mountainous ravine after a terrible landslide. The vehicle overturned, setting off live land mines and killing everyone inside.

Holbrooke, who had followed close behind, had the grim responsibility of returning his fallen colleagues for burial in Arlington Cemetery and reporting to the nation on their loss. In September, one month after burying his colleagues, Holbrooke flew back into Serbian hostile territory, more determined than ever to try to tame the inflamed tensions in Bosnia and Herzegovina.

However, he realized there was no place safe in Sarajevo to meet for negotiations. If the Americans were going to intervene, as the three warring countries indicated they must, the host location would have to be in a controlled setting in America. With the NATO forces forming a protective circle around the Croats, the Serbs suspended their aggression. The NATO suspension in bombing against the Serbs did not commence fully until a site for the peace talks had been determined. Code named Site X, the identity of the host location was not released until all nine parties were named and refereed.

A Dayton

Assistant secretary of state for administration Patrick F. Kennedy was tasked with scouting locations for the peace talks. The talks would have to occur on an American military base with amenities in which the three parties could live, interact, eat, work and relax in close quarters. The talks would be named the Balkan Proximity Peace Talks. Kennedy quickly narrowed the search to be presented to the president and to Warren Christopher down to three possible sites: the navy base at Newport, Rhode Island; Langley Air Force Base in Norfolk, Virginia; and Wright-Patterson Air Force Base (WPAFB) in Dayton, Ohio. Newport was eliminated; although it's amusing to think of Milošević wandering around the Breakers, the area was too spread out.[17] Langley was too close to Washington, D.C., and therefore too visible to the worldwide media. This was not supposed to be a vacation.

Kennedy met with Colonel Robbie Robinson, the wing commander from WPAFB, on October 18 to determine if WPAFB fit the State Department's needs. Kennedy had not been to WPAFB before but had been urged to check out the site, which is massive. Twenty-three thousand government personnel were assigned to WPAFB, with five visiting officers' quarters buildings grouped around a parking lot, only a few feet apart. The Hope Hotel and Conference Center provided a central location adjacent to the officers' quarters and would offer another meetinghouse. Although the rooms in the officers' buildings needed improvement, in all other ways, WPAFB fit the bill. The WPAFB was an easy one-hour flight to D.C. and would be far away from the media spotlight.

Colonel Robinson told Kennedy that the preparation of accommodations were a matter of civil engineering. He told Kennedy that they could knock out a few walls in the officers' buildings to create a suite of rooms for the dignitaries, adapt the electrical current for the EU alternating flow of electric current and set up redundant landline and Internet connectivity in each of the five buildings.

Kennedy told Colonel Robinson that if he could make this happen, he would stop looking for a different site. Colonel Robinson pulled in a group of commanders to prepare the installation, as he still needed to run the base while the transformation was going on. He also needed to get cooperation to help the State Department set up. A Department of Defense cooperative—such as WPAFB and the Department of State paired for a series of peace talks—was unprecedented. Robinson had not been asked to produce cross-coordinative results among military and diplomacy under similar terms at any other time in his career.

Dayton had two weeks to get ready.

News of the location of the Bosnian Proximity Peace talks didn't impress the European Union (EU) or the UN as a location to hold a major international peace conference. The Eighty-eighth Airbase Wing, with the adjacent Hope Hotel and Conference Center in area B, was no Camp David. The EU members were used to more opulent settings and more fanfare. "I do not want to be locked up like a monk in a fortress somewhere in Middle America," Milošević famously complained.

However, Holbrooke and Kennedy couldn't be more serious about Dayton. "[This was] to discourage Balkan warlords from running off to television studios in New York and Washington, D.C., every time the negotiations hit a snag. Dayton was a key point in establishing a neutral zone to conduct the talks. This WPAFB of Dayton, Ohio, was not chosen accidently. Pat Kennedy chose the location and saw five convenient officers' quarters buildings next to each other in the same wing," Holbrooke later said. The five-building visiting officers' accommodations provided each warring nation its own building, as well as ones for the Americans and the EU representative.[18]

Holbrooke needed the delegation to agree to a couple of contingencies before the entire entourage could make the trip to Dayton. He demanded the safe return of an American journalist who had skipped ahead of protocol and disappeared under the radar to film the Serbian atrocities. His sponsors had not approved the trip. Within days, the missing man was returned unharmed to the United States. The second criterion was that the Russian-controlled gas and electric power lines, piped into the Bosnian infrastructure, had to be turned back on. Millions of Bosnians were freezing at the start of the November 1995 peace talks. The Russians controlled the gas lines going into the country and claimed that the Bosnians owed them over $100 million in unpaid utilities. The Bosnians had no money to pay them. The Russians were told they had to agree to turn the services on and be paid later or there would be no Dayton.

The last stipulation was to arrest war criminals Karadzic and Mladić, the founder and leader of the separatist group that massacred the Bosniaks in Srebrenica, once the peace talks were over. Plus, these men were not to be given office in the reformed system of government. Otherwise, the deal would be null and void—no Dayton.

Vice President Al Gore said that Dayton was a gamble worth taking. Holbrooke had covered his bases. If the talks failed, a second wave of NATO bombings would begin immediately, with American troops' lives on the line and an upward cost of $2 billion.

The die were cast. The group would address as many issues as possible in the final agreements. What was not negotiated at Dayton would not be negotiated later. Milošević, Tuđman and Izetbegović consented to these terms. This was an all-or-nothing bid for peace.

Before the changeovers occurred at WPAFB, Colonel Robinson held a town hall meeting. WPAFB was the Department of Defense (DOD) and would need to assist the Department of State in a full-on capacity only until the talks started. Once negotiations had commenced, the responsibility, including media and menu service and recreation, fell to the Department of State. The Department of State was supported by Wes Clark, Holbrooke and the negotiations team. The department would handle security and the daily screening of media and visiting personnel.

The senior leaders at WPAFB were handpicked to manage the changeover through civil engineering. Captain Todd Emert was the executive officer at WPAFB and the security police squadron commander. The DOD and federal agencies began communications with supporting groups, such as the Defense Mapping Agency. This agency creates official maps. Tom Shoup and Al Schoolcraft were part of Eighty-eighth Air Base Wing host organization responsible for maintaining WPAFB. Other senior leaders and general officers were tenants at WPAFB. The Air Force Materiel Command owned the Eighty-eighth Air Base Wing and would support the State Department.

"The biggest problem was that we were Department of Defense and they were State Department. That is two different missions," said Robinson. "Schoolcraft ran the Mission Support Group and security police, the recreation services, Officer's club and Officer's quarters." Robinson found it easier to work with him under one umbrella to set up the campus.

He called in Schoolcraft to meet on that Saturday morning, the same day he met with Kennedy and the representative from the Department of Defense, Lieutenant General Farrell. Both leaders were scheduled to tour the base. Shoup worked on the civil engineering aspect in cooperation with the State Department twenty-four/seven to get the visiting officers' quarters ready. In two weeks' time, Shoup got the rooms ready to go. Civil engineers turned the five-building complex of officers' quarters into a compound with fences and a security shack. Shoup ensured all five buildings met the needs of all nine delegates. This included converting the electricity for the EU building from 110 volts to 220 volts.

"All the quarters were converted with back-up generators so as not to worry about the electricity going out," said Robinson.

Shoup got help from other government agencies—too numerous to name—such as the agency that handled security checkpoints. They fenced off the buildings, set up the VIP rooms and handled the construction. They tore out some of the walls to create two-room suites for some of the delegates, painted, put in new carpeting and doors and ordered five identical sets of furniture for each room in the buildings.

After a mid-point inspection of the five-plex, it was decided that a sidewalk from the five-plex to the Hope Hotel was needed because there was nothing but muddy earth between the Hope Hotel and the officers' quarters.

"Diplomats needed a curved sidewalk because they drink a lot," said Robinson. "This pathway to the Hope Hotel was the only curvy sidewalk poured in WPAFB. The walkway still exists today. It's its own attribution." WPAFB personnel planted a Peace Tree next to it.

To appease the French prime minister, Holbrooke agreed to draft the framework agreement in Dayton and then hold a formal signing ceremony in Paris one month later. Clinton would join the party in Dayton after a framework agreement was ready.

Shadow Diplomacy

The reaction in Dayton to hosting this diplomatic event was extraordinary. Most impressive to all the delegates was the warm greeting Daytonians gave them upon their arrival. WPAFB volunteers called every day asking how they could help. People lit candles in the windows. There was a peace ring that settled around the group. Christine Dull, co-founder of the Dayton International Peace Museum, played "Adagio" on her cello outside the base's fence line in tribute to Vedran Smailavoić. Smailović, a Sarajevo cellist, became a symbol of courage for playing in the city's bombarded streets for twenty-two days during its siege. The Bosnian cellist had played music in the streets of Sarajevo in protest of the killing of twenty-two Bosniaks, by mortar shell, while they were waiting in line for bread.

People would stop the Holbrooke team and tell them that they were praying for them.

Once the teams arrived in Dayton, the ambassadors were free to leave the compound anytime they were not working to sightsee, eat dinner at Kettering's four-star L'Aubèrge or enjoy basketball games in Indiana and Kentucky—something the people of Bosnia could not do.

During the day, the contact groups were expected to work together at the Hope Hotel and Conference Center and at the five barracks officers' quarters shared on the base. Accommodations were prepared with the idea that the delegates could live, work, eat, drink and discuss peace within the cordoned area. They could walk around to any of the buildings on the compound and talk. All activities and amenities were in proximity. The delegates had complete freedom in the fenced-in area, which was designed more to keep onlookers out.

Robinson insisted on greeting any presidents, prime ministers or senior diplomats who came and went. When Milošević, Tuđman and Izetbegović arrived, Robinson stuck out his hand and greeted them with "*Zdravo Kako ste*?" which means, "Hello how are you?" in Serbian. Milošević didn't answer right away; instead, he turned to his staff and talked hurriedly in Serbian to ask if Robinson could be trusted. The aid reassured him that, yes, as the base commander of the host environment, Robinson was OK. So the president tentatively shook Robinson's hand.

Robinson recalled some more of the distrust that came from the Balkan groups at the offset. When Robinson's crew set up the wiring to accommodate the EU voltage, they decided to get fire extinguishers. Civil engineering placed fire extinguishers in the officers' quarters in case of fire. Robinson knocked on one door of the advanced teams where the Europeans would be staying to offer them a fire extinguisher. Someone opened the door and put out a hand without stepping outside to take the fire extinguisher from him. Robinson traveled down the hall just a short way to another room and then turned around to see the fire extinguisher had been placed back into the hallway outside the door.

"Whoever it was who opened the door didn't trust that the fire extinguisher wouldn't be bugged," said Robinson.

The Dayton Model for peace turned out to be less official business than group therapy in a military wing. Several rooms at the Hope Hotel were set up—some larger and some smaller—to hold individual discussions and negotiations. There was a short drive to the officers' club, where the base served quail, venison and pheasant—popular cuisine for people from the Balkans. The officers' club was a part of the proximity, as was the base operations to fly in media on location. Packy's, the restaurant inside the Hope Hotel and Conference Center—named after comedian Bob Hope—was turned over to the negotiating and media team.

A type of shadow diplomacy went on behind the scenes to support the delegates' mission. John McCance, who served as senior public affairs officer, was assigned to provide direct support to under secretary of state R. Nicolas Burns. McCance's responsibilities included overseeing all aspects of logistics and air force public affairs support for Secretary Burn during the

The officers' club at the WPAFB was built in 1917 as part of Wright Field. *Courtesy of U.S. Department of the Army.*

negotiations at the Hope Hotel, which was the principal negotiation site. Additionally, McCance maintained constant communication with other senior air force public affairs officers to ensure some three hundred–plus news media representatives were alerted to and moved, if necessary, for Department of State daily press briefings. Part of his shadow diplomacy was going from building to building to make the delegates' stay a more pleasant experience. McCance was in charge of delegate security, travel routes, menu and nutritional selections and recreational schedules.

McCance hired the personnel, signed up reservists and scheduled them the days they were available to work. He organized and scheduled the Work Out Media Center's security forces and provided bomb-sniffing dogs. McCance would register each member of the media every day and run a security sweep. As director of public affairs, McCance had to decide if he wanted to alert the media every time there was movement.

"The effort put forth by the Base Wing Command at WPAFB was transparent to the delegates of the State Department, including Pat Kennedy, and Holbrooke," said Robinson. "These people recognized the work being done." The White House advanced team, the staff of the American delegates, showed up early and saw the amended area.

Colonel Robinson said the base had to call off the bomb-sniffing dogs once the dignitaries arrived. "I will not be sneefed," the French ambassador told him. Holbrooke apologized to the ambassador, and Robinson called off the dogs. Security was not as tight in 1995, before 9/11. After 9/11, bomb-sniffing dogs would have been mandatory. Robinson wanted to keep everybody happy—it was part of his job.

On November 1, the first day of negotiations, the delegates were met with a red carpet greeting from the WPAFB Honor Guard. Two flatbed tractor-trailers were butted up against each other and plywood was laid across. This was the riser for the TV cameras. The cameras were set up eight feet from the tractor. When the principals came in, the press would shoot down on spectators and interview the delegates.

"We are here to give Bosnia and Herzegovina a chance to be a country at peace, not a killing field," Warren Christopher said during the opening night ceremonies.

The talks went, day by day, from the hours of 9:00 a.m. to 9:00 p.m. The restaurant, Packy's, was off-limits to the public and reserved for State Department use only. Sometimes the group met in the officers' quarters or at Packy's. McCance would travel to the different buildings and look at the maps posted outside the officials' rooms, day by day, as the representatives hashed out borders and division of land. One bit of territory would be marked off with a marker or tape. This showed the progress from where the discussions had been for the day.

On November 11, Veterans Day, Croatian president Tuđman wanted to go over to the National Museum of the United States Air Force to lay a wreath in remembrance. Robertson recounted:

> *Tuđman said he really appreciated what the air force did to liberate the country and to honor the air force's effort in World War II to get the Nazis out of the area. For the first half of discussion on peace, the talks bore the name the Balkan Proximity Peace Talks. By the time the General Framework for Peace was initialed on November 21, the Balkan Proximity Peace Talks had become the Dayton Peace Accords, in homage to the community of Dayton's involvement at such an extent for an historic event—an event that might have gone unattended in a larger city.*

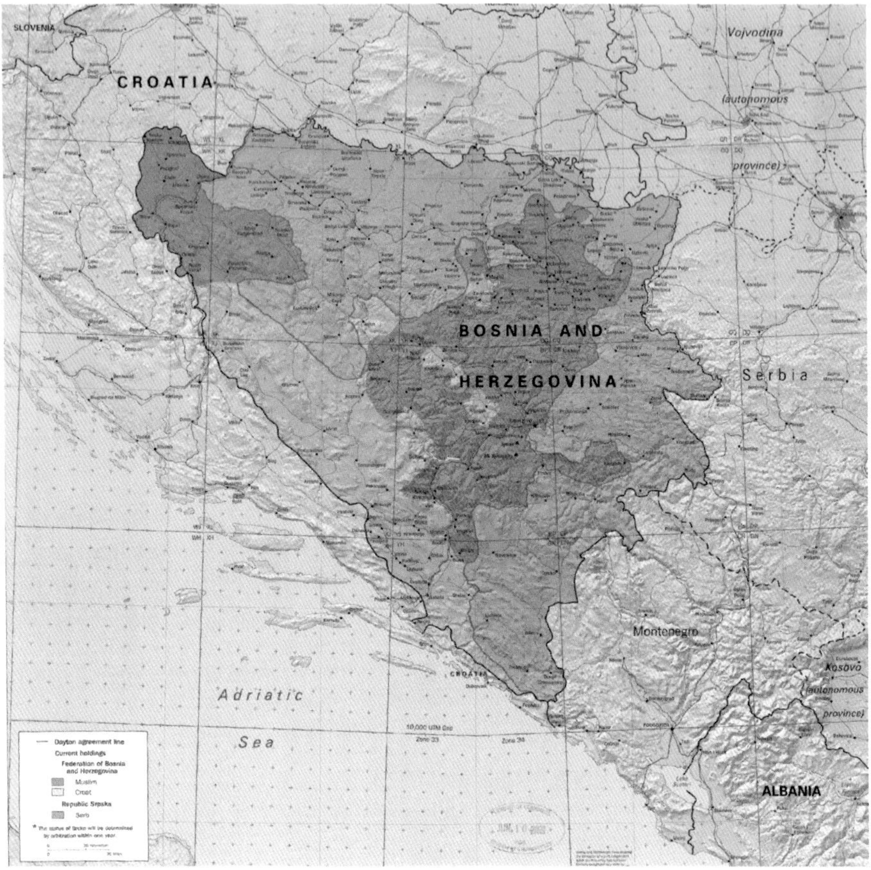

A map of Bosnia and Herzegovina was produced to support the treaty accord from Dayton. *Courtesy of General Philip W. Nuber, director of the Defense Mapping Agency, 1996.*

The General Framework Agreement for Peace consisted of eleven supporting annexes with maps. The accords had several major goals: one, the ending of hostilities; two, the authorization of military and civilian programs going into effect; three, the establishment of a central Bosnian government; and four, excluding individuals convicted by the International War Crimes Tribunals from taking part in the running of that government. The Implementation Force's (IFOR) specific role was to implement the military annexes of the General Framework Agreement for Peace (GFAP) in Bosnia and Herzegovina under a one-year mandate from December 20, 1995, to December 20, 1996, under the codename Operation Joint Endeavour. IFOR is made up of NATO countries that would police the region for any uprising one year after the General Framework Agreement was signed.

As a result of the negotiations, Bosnian Serbs got large tracts of mountainous territories back—4 percent of Bosnian Croats' land and some small amounts from Bosniaks. However, they were pressured to surrender Sarajevo and some vital Eastern Bosnian/Herzegovina positions. By changing quality to quantity of land, their percentage shrank from 49 to 48 percent after Milošević gave Croatia the Brcko District. The Serbs actually gained a little bit more land than the 46 percent they owned prior to Dayton. The Bosniaks got most of Sarajevo and some important positions in eastern Bosnia and Herzegovina. The Bosniaks' percentage grew from 28 percent prior to Dayton to 30 percent. Large tracts of prewar Bosniak- and Bosnian Croat–inhabited lands remained under Bosnian Serb control. Bosnian Croats gave up the most land to the Bosnian Serbs but agreed to set up a municipality afterward. All five contact groups' foreign ministers and the leaders of all three countries had formally agreed to a 51/49 percent split of Bosnian territory between the federation and the Bosnian Serbs.

A huge dispute in setting up this treaty nearly cost the negotiations.

The Final Hour

The final day for the negotiations among the contact groups shaved off 1 percent of the map of land in Bosnia and Herzegovina to make concessions to Croatia. However, it was not discovered until late in the night—after twenty-two straight hours—that President Izetbegović of BiH was left out of the last-minute negotiations with Milošević for the final border approval. It was prime minister of Bosnia and Herzegovina Silajdzic who cut the deal with Milošević and Tuđman—not the Croatian president. It was an oversight that nearly blew apart the Dayton Peace Talks.

McCance recalls the spiraling of events from the arrival of the White House advance team. Colonel Robinson was met in the ballroom of the Hope Hotel with twenty people sitting in the chair; Colonels Schoolcraft and Kirkwood were there.

The White House advance team had been there all afternoon, waiting. It was still daylight. One of the State Department delegates from the Washington team, who still works for the Clinton Foundation, was traveling from the Far East. WPAFB was her first stop in the United States in about three weeks. She asked McCance for a pack of cigarettes and a pair of pantyhose, certain that they would have to make a statement. The air was expectant with anticipation. Something was about to happen.

McCance went home at 2:00 a.m. and showered but didn't sleep. He got up, put on a fresh uniform and was told negotiations had broken down upon his return. Holbrooke canceled President Clinton's visit. "He was supposed to be here on November 20," said Robinson. "However, the Croats walked out that night and communications broke down." Warren Christopher had packed his bags. This was the longest day of negotiation and the longest day of McCance's career.

"Everyone was so invested in seeing this become successful: all the work that the base had done to prepare accommodations for the delegates. The hope that Clinton was coming from the White House, and that we were going to witness history at WPAFB—knowing that this was all going to fall apart," said McCance. "Christopher had gone on talks in the American building with the delegates for twenty-two hours, without stopping, and negotiations had failed. The supporting State Department personnel and the base command stayed in a holding pattern all day long."

Well into the night in the American building of the WPAFB, the smell of pizza and California chardonnay drifted into the hallway. Holbrooke recounted the evening's events:

> *Milošević stuck out his hand. Slightly surprised, Silajdzic took it. Except for some details, the deal was done. BiH and Croatia had agreed upon the final slice of territory. It was 4 AM 22 hours in. For a moment, we were silent, too stunned to react. They talked with sudden ease, and, for the first time, joked. Silajdzic seemed euphoric at his negotiating triumph. Milošević was relieved that it was over. Christopher went outside and asked Bob Bradke, his faithful executive assistant, to fetch a bottle of his favorite wine from the supply with which he always traveled. Out of plastic cups, we drank to peace. (Holbrooke wrote that Silajdzic, a practicing Muslim, drank a Coke.) An Air Force photographer came in to record the triumphant scene. Overlooked, Izetbegović had slept through the last stages of negotiations.*
>
> *After a drink or two, Silajdzic went off to get Izetbegović, who showed up in his pajamas. In negotiating the final 51/49 split, all of Silajdzic's "givebacks "were from Croat-controlled territory—and no Croatians were present to approve the finalization of borders. Silajdzic and Sacirbey, both Prime Minister and Foreign Minister of Croatia respectively could assist in discussion and initial the signoff, however, the final approval of any agreement would have to be verified by President Izetbegović. Izetbegović,*

> *Silajdzic, and Sacirbey sat in the room waiting for us. Christopher and I took up our usual places next to each other on the couch, and Christopher tried to appeal to President of Croatia Izetbegović.*

Holbrooke said:

> *"Mr. President, we have come a long way in Dayton, and we are very close to a successful conclusion. If you will reduce by one percent the amount of land you claim, we can make a final deal. You do not have to give up any land that you currently control. It's a very good Deal, Mr. President. We have obtained almost everything you asked for." The president was inconsolable. He mentioned the city of Brcko several times. He felt that had become the object of all the pressure at Dayton. His delegation was about to explode.*

Christopher said:

> *Mr. President, I am truly disappointed at the fuzzy, unrealistic, and sloppy manner in which you and your delegation have approached this negotiation. You can have a successful outcome, or not, as you wish. But we must have your answer in one hour. If you say no we will announce in the morning that the Dayton peace talks have been closed down.*

"Not suspended," Holbrooke added, "closed down. In one hour." The rest of the group went back to the Hope Hotel for a one-hour nap. Silajdzic countered in a towering rage. "You have ruined everything! Don't you know that we can never give in to an American ultimatum?" Holbrooke rounded up his last father-knows-best approach for one more intervention.

"You are the ones that ruined it," Holbrooke said. "You have 95 percent of what you wanted and you are about to piss it all away because you can't get your own act together." Silajdzic tried to argue, but Holbrooke told him to leave. "Use the next hour to get your president to accept this offer and the war will be over. You will not regret it."

A few minutes later, Milošević quietly came forward in an aside to Holbrooke and said, "I will walk the final mile for peace. I will agree to the arbitration at Brcko one year from now."

The final offer from the Serbs was to put the District of Brcko under arbitration for one year. Seven hundred journalists were waiting outside the Hope Center to hear from Holbrooke. Outside the conference room, Sacirbey broke the news that the spirited talks were over and the

Corporal Pogyre Markovic and Captain Joseph Fisher planted a black pine tree in September 2010 in the Topolovo region of Montenegro. *Courtesy of U.S. Air Force.*

peacemakers had reached an agreement. Christopher and Holbrooke were to make the announcement to the press at 10:00 a.m. Brcko, a city of forty-one thousand, would become part of the federal entity, a special district outside the jurisdiction of the Federation of Bosnia and Herzegovina and the RS.

Izetbegović said, "It's not a just peace." He paused. "But my people need peace."

American General Clark and Izetbegović sat down and drew up the map that would finalize the 51/49 split of the territory. When Milošević heard that Izetbegović had accepted his offer of Brcko, there were tears in his eyes.[19] After so much death, now there would be peace.

McCance was called over the radio to bring champagne to the American delegation room, down the curvy sidewalk. The president made the announcement at 11:40 a.m. from the Rose Garden. This speech almost did not happen.

"After nearly four years, 250,000 people killed, 2 million refugees and atrocities that appalled people all over the world, the people of Bosnia finally have a chance to turn from the horror of war to the promise of peace," the president said. Closing ceremonies were held on the following Tuesday afternoon.

In an afterword, the draft of the peace talks occurred on November 21, 1995. The Dayton Peace Accords were officially signed in Paris, France, on December 14, 1995, one month later. The signees were president of Serbia Slobodan Milošević; first chairman of the presidency of BiH Alija Izetbegović; president of Croatia Franjo Tuđman; President Bill Clinton; president of France Jacques Chirac; British prime minister John Major; chancellor of Germany Helmut Kohl; and Russian prime minister Viktor Chernomyrdin.

The Agreement

The 1995 Dayton Peace Accords divided Bosnia into two semi-independent states: the Federation of Bosnia and Herzegovina, inhabited mainly by Bosnian Muslims and Bosnian Croats, and the Serb-dominated RS. Each region has its own government controlling taxation, educational policy and even foreign policy. Financial aid totaling $14 billion was flown in from seventeen different foreign governments, eighteen UN agencies, twenty-seven intergovernmental organizations and about two hundred nongovernmental organizations (NGOs). IFOR troops and other peacekeeping armies were brought in to police the region. The General Framework Agreement is concurred to be a politically top-heavy and expensive solution to operate, but it has kept the peace for twenty years.

"Most peace talks do end with very little accomplished. Not much is gained, usually. How many times have we met with Iran? If Dayton failed, this model would have been proven a failure, despite our best efforts. The big surprise to Dayton and to the diplomatic community was that it actually worked," said Robinson. Six months later, Robinson was assigned to Edwards Air Force Base to be a test pilot. His linkage to the State Department was limited after that. Now retired, he recalled that no other similar effort had come together in his entire career.

"We have heard from several people from Bosnia over the years just how important the Dayton Peace Accords were to them," said Robinson. "At the time, we had no idea how things would eventually turn out, but it was worth the effort. I just hope that someone can find a way to use the Accords as a template for future peace talks."

Colonel Robinson received a nice thank-you letter, signed by Secretary of State Christopher, who was very impressed that WPAFB was able to pull off the transformation in just under two weeks. He told him that he couldn't get this kind of output done in one year in Washingoton, D.C.

"The team that came together across the base and the Dayton community and the other agencies that came together across the federal government was really impressive," added Robinson. "I am truly impressed at how they understood the mission's importance and were prepared to do what it took to accommodate this measure for peace."

A copy of the final map from the Defense Mapping Agency to commemorate the Dayton Peace Accords is set to be donated for permanent display at the Dayton International Peace Museum.

6

DIVERSITY

IMMIGRANTS FROM THE 1990S

Dayton is not a gateway city like Miami, Florida, or New York City, but it has become an immigrant-friendly city. Between 2000 and 2010, the general population of the Miami Valley has decreased by 15 percent and has seen 50 percent growth in immigrant population. Today, roughly 4 percent of the entire population of the Miami Valley is foreign born. The main reason for the leap in the past decade is the increase in number of refugees assigned to live in the United States or other UN-controlled nations. The top five countries of origin for new citizens that call Dayton home are Turkey, Russia, India, the Philippines and Mexico. Many come to Dayton and the United States in search of a fresh start. Others come to Dayton for career opportunities or to be nearer to family.

Some of the Dayton immigrant communities who have come to the United States under refugee status are from Turkey, Rwanda, Burundi, Iraq and Ethiopia. During 2011 and 2012, the Refugee Resettlement Program of Catholic Social Services of the Miami Valley (CSSMV) received 144 refugees for resettlement services. Newly arrived refugees in Dayton receive supportive services from CSSMV's Refugee Resettlement Program and are placed in furnished housing and given a cultural orientation overview, employment assistance and linkage to community resources, such as referral to English as a second language services and medical services.

Many immigrants come to this city seeking a familiar community and find warm neighbors, a low cost of living and a rebounding job market. As a result of the increase in immigration, Dayton has seen a growth in start-up and smaller businesses and community revitalization. This diversity has infused new life into Dayton neighborhoods and has contributed to the growth and the vitality of the city.

Diversity has become an intrinsic part of Dayton's peace heritage. Part of the community pride for foreign-born, as well as naturalized, Daytonians is having the opportunity to exchange culture. The International Festival, or the World A'Fair, held at the Dayton Convention Center at the end of May every year, was introduced in 1973 to celebrate culture from around the world.

The South Slavic Club

In 1973, the South Slavic Club (SSC) was introduced by a University of Dayton priest, Father Rus, formerly of Slovenia. At once to edify Dayton, Father Rus organized the World A'Fair, as well as the Dayton Lebanese Festival, held at St. Ignatius Church, both beginning that same year.

The purpose of the SSC was simply to celebrate the history, topography, literature, art, music, drama, language and popular culture associated with the former Republics of Yugoslavia, including Bosnia-Herzegovina, Croatia, Macedonia, Serbia-Montenegro, Slovenia and Bulgaria. Many of those belonging to this group are second-, third- or fourth-generation Slavic Americans and have no current political or familial ties to their country of origin. The overall purpose of the club is not focused on religion or politics but to simply enjoy the culture.

The SSC has over one hundred members in Dayton. SSC president John Pappas said the community members began arriving as a group in Dayton and throughout Ohio in the late nineteenth and early twentieth centuries—just before World War I. "The South Slavic Club is a social organization, not a political organization," said Pappas. "One of the goals is to provide opportunities for the Dayton community to experience the music, dances and cultures of the region." The SSC asserts that it is not necessary to have cultural ties to the Balkans to become a club member.

"We have several different cultures within our group, including Romas, or gypsy customs," said Jim Rohal, first vice-president of the SSC. "The club sponsors many such dances, dinners and music groups throughout the year, which are open to the community." A popular form of circle or folk dancing, called Kolo dancing, was introduced. "None of the Kolo dances require partners," Rohal said "Probably half of our dancers, including me, aren't Slav. We're there for our love of the dancing and an interest in the culture. We just wanted to assure you that you won't feel like an outsider if you come."

The group's activities throughout the year are open to the community. Zivio grew from the SSC's adult in-house dance group that has formed over the years and has performed at eclectic recitals at the World A'Fair.[20]

The Dayton Lebanese Church

With the city's Muslim population swelling to encompass nearly 10 percent of the Dayton city population, Dayton has welcomed diversity into its borders. Some native-born people of Dayton expressed concern over the thinning job market or other potentially negative effects from the surge in the immigrant population. However, the city has chosen instead to adopt an open-door policy to immigrants of diverse cultural backgrounds. City commissioner Matt Joseph, a second-generation immigrant born of Lebanese parents, has fortified efforts to help Dayton become more inclusive to foreign-born peoples.

Joseph said many Muslims or peoples of Middle Eastern descent face discrimination in Dayton and the United Sates because of the continuing Middle East conflicts. St. Ignatius of Antioch Maronite Catholic Church, led by Father Guy Sarkis, sponsors the Dayton Lebanese Festival, which offers the Dayton community a chance to experience Middle East culture firsthand from countries such as Syria, Iraq, Iran and Lebanon. The St. Ignatius parish has an estimated sixty families of direct Middle Eastern descent in its congregation and invites the community to attend its bilingual services, which feature a Eucharistic prayer, taught in English and ancient Armamic—the language spoken at the time of Christ. With these family connections still intact, many of these parishioners are able make many trips to the Holy Lands to bring back authentic merchandise to sell at the Lebanese Festival and the World A'Fair, including lanterns, candles, hookahs and hip-scarves. Attendees can expect over a dozen carnival rides, craft booths and several musical acts, including belly dancers. Menu items are prepared from scratch in the parish kitchen.

"The most important thing for Americans to realize is there are good people from the Middle East and they have a good time like everybody else," church elder Trish Zennie said. "These people believe in God. They're not terrorists. There is a mixture of Middle Eastern nationalities with family connections. The church is open to all people here and abroad."[21]

The Ahiska Turks

Community leaders have agreed that Turkish immigrants and refugees have taken pride of ownership in their new city. Since the UN opened up refugee status for the Ahiska Turks in 2004, 530 Turkish émigrés and their families have joined the Dayton community. Upon their arrival, the Turks have turned the neighborhood around. They have fixed up over five hundred abandoned structures in Old North Dayton and Riverside areas—around Stanley, Webster and Linden Streets—for a modest cost of $20,000 to $30,000 each. Many have opened up smaller business, which has helped to bring Dayton back from its post auto industry slump. City officials, such as former mayor Gary Leitzell, have encouraged the continued arrival of the Turkish immigrants and their families. However, it was not an easy road for any of them to get here.

The Ahiska Turks, who originated from Russia, shared a centuries' old history with their neighbors in Turkey. In a secret maneuver in 1944, Joseph Stalin deported over 115,000 Meskhetian, or Ahiska, Turks from their native Georgia deep into Central Asia—the Kazakhstan, Kyrgyzstan and Uzbekistan regions. Over 40,000 of the deportees died from extreme cold and dehydration that first winter. However, this forced eviction was publically denied by the Soviet Union until 1968. Although no official explanation for the deportation was given, it was rumored that Stalin was paranoid that the Muslim Ahiska Turks would be disloyal to the Soviet Union should the Soviets attempt to attack Turkey. However, the worst was yet to come.

The Ahiska Turks were not counted in the Soviet census and, thus, were not recognized as Turkish citizens upon the dissolution of the Union of the Soviet Socialist Republic (USSR). At the fall of communism, the local authorities, such as the Krasnodar, conveniently blamed the Ahiska Turks for the economic fallout—a situation the latter did not help to create.

"When the Soviet Union was unraveling and going to hell in central Asia, the Ahiska Turks were killed and persecuted," said Adil Baguirov,

Dayton Board of Education and Ahiska Turks American Community Center member. "There were some that attempted to go back home, but the Georgian houses had long been occupied by other owners."

In June 1989, Uzbek extremists took part in a mass slaughter of the surviving deportees. Without a country to claim them, the Ahiska Turks were defenseless. An estimated nine thousand Ahiska Turks have been admitted to the United States since 2004. Unlike the Turks, who are typical immigrants who must apply their own resources for the move, refugees such as the Ahiska Turks usually own nothing but the clothes on their backs. The United States, as well as other supporting members of the UN, will supply refugees with small loans, Medicaid and food stamps to emigrate.

Once removed from their native country, organizations such as the Turkish American Society of Ohio (TASO) have stepped in to help Turks adapt to American life, particularly in Ohio. According to Director Ozgur Ozey, TASO, which is a member of the Turkish American Alliance, has also successfully sponsored a number of educational and student trips to help Turks reconnect with their cultural identities. TASO is a nonprofit organization founded in 2008, which replaced Scioto Educational Foundation (SEF) in 2010.

The Ahiska Turkish American Community Center (ATACC) was founded and run by president Isolom Shakhbandarov. The Turks and the Ahiska Turks of Russia often schedule joint social and educational activities through TASO and the ATACC as a way of community bonding.

Shakhbandarov was encouraged by Dayton's warm reception on immigration. However, he believes immigrants appreciate freedoms that Americans often take for granted. He said:

> *The U.S. granted us refugee status to save us. In Russia, Turks would be beaten up or denied opportunities. No State ID was allowed because they were denied citizenship. One could not own or sell anything. The old Soviet documents would not allow Ahiska Turks to immigrate, or go to school. If one had to drive a car he or she would have to bribe authorities to proceed. Life was hell every single day. The U.S. is a great country, however, the power that controls most of the world needs to be up to date. This is the best government—the best democracy—in the world, but voter turnout is very low.*[22]

Burundi Drummers

The Republic of Burundi is a country located in eastern Africa in the middle of Rwanda, Tanzania and the Democratic Republic of the Congo. A very tiny country of just 10,745 square miles, its size is an area that is slightly bigger than Massachusetts and just under the size of Hawaii.

With a population of slightly over 8.5 million, the country is known for being one of the five poorest in the world, with civil wars and corruption abounding. It's also said to be the "Switzerland of Africa" due to its year-round green scenery and many rolling hills.

Dieudonne Nsabimana arrived in the United States from Bujumbura, Burundi, in 2008 and joined his wife, who was residing in Dayton at the time. The couple lives in Dayton with their three children. Nsabimana works for the CSSMV. This contact enables him to stay involved in the inner African community while helping newly arrived refugees settle in Dayton. Through his work, many get the opportunity to obtain an education, as well as receive additional free services.

Nsabimana has worked diligently on improving the lives of the Burundian youth since 2008. He has recognized the value of introducing and teaching Burundian culture to the Dayton community. By acknowledging and promoting the importance of his culture, he has created and introduced the Burundian Drum Line and a female dance group, which have become some of Dayton's favorite performances to watch. He has created the organization called the Burundian Cultural and Educational Association (BCEA).

"The introduction of the Burundian drummers and dance performances were important for our Burundian youth. Most of our youth were born in refugee camps and have never returned to Burundi to learn about our culture. The Burundian drummers and women dance performance group can teach our youth about our culture and traditions," said Nsabimana.

These performances were a part of important ceremonies within the kingdom, such as births, funerals and the enthronement of the king of Burundi from the sixteenth century. A unique drum ceremony, called *Umuganuro*, allowed the king to bless the plants and produce a bountiful harvest.[23]

Asian, Indian and Latino Residents Impress the Importance of Education

The six most populous Asian groups in the Dayton area are: Chinese, Asian Indian, Japanese, Korean, Filipino and Vietnamese. According to the 2010 U.S. census, there are 141,761 people living in the city of Dayton, 2 percent of whom are Asian. Dayton-area Asian entrepreneurs represent 2.2 percent of the total Miami Valley–owned businesses. Sponsored and hosted through the Wright State University (WSU) Asian/Hispanic/Native American Center (AHNA), Asian history and culture is celebrated in April, during Asian history month, honoring the Asian American influence on Dayton.

Among the AHNA dedicated faculty is WSU mathematics professor Munsup Seoh. Seoh believes that, overall, the city's Asian population is underrepresented. As one-time secretary, chair of the board of trustees, treasurer and president of the Dayton Area Korean Association (DAKA), Seoh and other community leaders have spearheaded education and outreach. The DAKA, in coordination with the AHNA, is heavily involved in community events throughout the year, not just in April. Originally from Kyung-Ju, Korea, Seoh joined WSU's faculty in 1983. The DAKA's work is supported and promoted by many independently owned businesses and ten of the local churches.[24]

As a continuing part of the celebration of Asian heritage, the AHNA remains focused on education and the development of youth leadership in the areas of conflict resolution, cultural awareness and the historical contribution of American Asians. The AHNA launched the youth ambassadors program beginning with the 2015–16 school year. Called the E3! Ambassadors program, this effort allows youth to coordinate with the federal government to brainstorm on improvements for quality of life for Asian Americans in education and mental health and provides pathways to public service and immigration. The E3! Ambassadors were selected from twenty-nine different cities and have hosted about fifty-five events. The Asian American Council of Dayton, founded in 2002, promotes participation in democratic processes and works in conjunction with groups such as the AHNA and DAKA.

The Asian American Council continues to support federal, state and local legislation that protects the civil rights of all U.S. residents. As part of its ongoing mission, the DAKA, in coordination with the Asian American Council, discourages the use of stereotypes and not just against Asians. The AHNA typically promotes activities that support common interests, such as the World A'Fair or the annual march on the Martin Luther King Jr. holiday or sponsoring mathematics competitions or essay contests. Many have spoken on behalf of Muslims who faced discrimination in America post 9/11.

As part of a special event, Dayton's PBS station, channel 16's ThinkTV®, partnered with the AHNA of WSU and produced a documentary, broadcast in April 2015, which commemorated the fortieth anniversary of the fall of Saigon. This documentary, entitled *Between Two Worlds*, recounted seven Dayton-area Vietnamese survivors' ordeals during the invasion of South Vietnam by the Viet Cong—called the People's Army of Vietnam and the National Liberation Front—on April 30, 1975.

Tariq Ahmad

Better employment or advantages in education are usually what drive an immigrant to leave his or her country of origin. The country of India is no exception. Sometimes Asian Indians are able to make a move to America with family sponsorship. Sometimes it is through the promise of employment.[25] According to 2010 census data, Asian Indians represent 34.00 percent of the Dayton region's Asian population and between 0.06 and 1.50 percent of the overall population of the Miami Valley. The India club of Dayton, the primary social networking source of the Dayton Asian Indian community, does not promote religious or political views and is focused primarily on career and social assimilation for the Asian Indian immigrant.

India native Tariq Ahmad came to the United States as the owner of the Tim Horton's on Needmore Road. He made the choice to move to Canada from India to obtain his education on a student visa. There, he worked for fifteen years as a degreed lab research scientist studying hematology and chemistry. After marrying a Canadian citizen and starting a family, Ahmad bought a restaurant franchise from Tim Horton's. He had wanted to get a franchise in Canada, however, more stores were opening up in the United States at the time. If he did have a choice of location in the United States, he would have moved the family to New York. With regard to Tim Horton's placement of his business franchise in Ohio, "It was love it or leave it."

Tim Horton's picked the location for him. Once the store was ready, he was granted an E2 business visa to open the Dayton store. Today, he is still a

Canadian citizen, and as a Canadian citizen, some restrictions still apply. He can visit anywhere in the United States but cannot work in the United States, except for the Canadian-owned Tim Horton's.

Ahmad found coming to Dayton was a nice surprise. The cost of living in Dayton is far better than in Canada. "People are so open here, and we never felt like we were unwelcome," he said.

David Yeh

Asian-owned businesses in Ohio have sales and receipts of $7.3 billion annually. David Yeh said he and his family came to the United States in the 1980s for educational opportunities. First landing in Chicago at Northwestern, the eldest of Yeh's three uncles came to the Chicago area on a student visa. He maintained a 3.8 to 4.0 grade point average and won enough scholarships to pay for his studies. The rest of the family came over in 1990 and moved to Dayton because it was closer to Yeh's father's eldest brother, who was established in the educational field. The uncle earned a PhD and became a professor at the University of Kentucky. Yeh's father was the last of the three brothers to migrate. Yeh was eleven at the time.

Although his uncle excelled academically, Yeh said it took him more than two years to speak colloquial English with most of the kids in his class at school. Language was problematic at first because of the different language rules. He was not taught American English in his foreign language classes at school, which might have helped him adapt easier. He said now, overseas, American English is a very popular language to study.

Yeh found that it is also harder for Americans to pronounce foreign-sounding names. When he immigrated to the United States with his father, he changed his first name to David to fit in. Yeh said that he generally does not give out his Chinese name because of the difficulty Americans have in pronouncing it. Yeh does feel that he has had the opportunity, however, to retain much of his homeland's culture in Dayton. Many local Chinese or Asian churches celebrate Chinese holidays, and there are a few community-wide festivals that introduce Chinese culture, such as the International Festival.

A valuable resource for local Chinese immigrants wishing to connect culturally is the Dayton Chinese American Association, or the DACA. The DACA was the starter of the Chinese community, and most of the founding members are Taiwanese. Yeh discovered that there were two different Dayton

Chinese communities after he came to the area: one religious and the other academic. There is a Taiwanese church on Indian Ripple Road and a rich culture of Chinese students at Wright State and the University of Dayton.

The culture of Dayton-area Chinese, to date, is a mix of all types of professional people. Since the 1990s, more Taiwanese than Chinese have moved into the area. Many Chinese immigrants have come over to the country as air force civilian or pilots. After achieving their education in the United States, many follow their parents and go back to Taiwan. Yeh has encountered quite a few Chinese from the DACA who have returned home. Yeh said Asian immigrants from countries such as Laos and Cambodia came over to the United States on refugee status and are not likely to return to their home countries.

"The youngest generation has the experience with American culture that makes it easier to soak up the knowledge," Yeh said. "For the older generation adaptation was a little more trouble." Yeh visits his family over in China "once in a blue moon." He has family on mother's side in China. When he visits his homeland, his mother's family tells him he speaks with a Taiwanese accent.

Entrepreneur Juan Ubrieta Beautifies East Third

Latino-owned businesses in Ohio have generated an annual revenue of $2.3 billion through 2014. The purchasing power of Ohio's Latino population was $7.7 billion in 2014. Juan Ubrieta, chief executive officer of Ubrieta Construction, came to the United States in 1985 to build something special here and found his community pride. Gifted with a passion for historical renovation, remodeling and home improvement, Ubrieta—originally from Guanajuato, Mexico—arrived in Dayton with a dream to start his own construction business and a goal to become successful in America. He became a United States citizen in 1992 and has developed an impeccable reputation for remodeling and construction. A building at 1725 East Third Street was gutted by a devastating fire in the late '90s. Ubrieta saw potential in this building that had become an eyesore in the neighborhood, purchased it and completely remodeled it to upscale standards, even revitalizing the woodwork and hand painting a mural on the stairwell.

Ubrieta specializes in custom design and is equipped to re-create the exact molding of original woodwork in Dayton historical homes. His meticulous craftsmanship resembles "a timeless way of building" rather than rote, timely construction. His reputation has followed him with each build throughout the cities of Dayton and Oakwood—and he is featured in the *Oakwood Register*. Rental organizations, he said, that utilize his services just give him the work order and the leeway to create something masterful. Generally, he said, "they don't ask what the cost will be." Most of the jobs are referrals on kitchen and bathroom home remodeling.

Ubrieta added a mill shop to the back of his storefront on East Third to accomplish the detail essentials necessary to restore historical properties. This handiwork is what has made his contract services so sought after and unique to the city of Dayton at large. To cut his custom designs, Ubrieta creates profiles for existing molds to build exact duplicates of the woodwork. In addition to home remodel and construction, Ubrieta has accumulated twenty rental properties to date for remodel and rental expansion throughout the East Third Street Business District. Intent on seeing this community strive toward excellence, Ubrieta was mindful of not only doing good work but also living well.

As Ubrieta built and established his business, his ideals grew to evolve around family and mentoring young people. He found kids to be an inspiration in his line of work—they're the future. "Kids need a place to feel safe; a place that is theirs." He said kids need to feel like somebody cares for them. "I have seen so many people in the area and can see that they don't love their kids. Kids today are looking for love," he said. "See, family cohesion is a problem. Mom and dad work too much—they have no time to sit down and talk to kids."

"This country gave me the opportunity to be what I am today," he said. "If I can come here and do it, so can you."

7

HEALING THE COMMUNITY THROUGH MEDIATION

There is a community peace work in Dayton that has been well established through mediation and community dialogue. Dayton has become a model for restorative justice through the Dayton Mediation Center. Tom Walrab—peace volunteer, social activist and retired director for the city of Dayton's Human Relations Council (HRC)—said that Dayton is a community that excels in civic engagement, or the act of bringing people together to support one another. Transformative mediation is a 360-degree method to open community dialogue between disagreeing parties.

The Dayton Mediation Center's (DMC) mission is to help promote compassionate mediation and restorative justice procedures using transformative mediation methods with trained, community volunteer mediators. Transformative mediation was first adopted as a peaceful alternative for Dayton- and Montgomery County–area residents' response and resolution to conflict without involving a third-party authority or litigator.

KYLEN ENGLISH

In a well-publicized case from 2011, court mediation was recommended. Dayton police documented the apparent suicide of a teenager named Kylen English, who kicked his way out of a police cruiser. Although English perished in police custody, there was no sustainable evidence to implicate

The Salem Avenue Business District, a district that was listed on the National Register of Historic Places, was part of the Steele's Hill–Grafton Hill Business District built in West Dayton in the early twentieth century. *Courtesy of the Historic American Buildings Survey, 1933.*

the Dayton city police. "Police are shooting black males throughout the country," said Walrab. "How do we lock arms as a community?"

DMC's transformative mediation services allowed parties from the victim's family and the police to come together to express their grief and distress after the tragedy.

In the following documentation supported by the actual video footage and audio recordings from the police cruiser, a young man who had been picked up for harassing his ex-girlfriend that evening grew overly agitated. The girlfriend had reported inappropriate behavior for up to several months leading up to the event. The following is a paraphrased excerpt of recorded events chronicled by the *Dayton Daily News*. The staff writers were Ken-Yon Hardy, Vickie Harris and Patty Marcano.

At 7:30 p.m. on July 16, 2011, Dayton police officers Travis Salyer and Alex Magill respond to a 911 call at a house in the College Hill neighborhood, on Yale Avenue, about a reported burglary in progress. The female complainant said that a black male tried to break into her apartment. She told police that English was her niece's ex-boyfriend. The niece, aged sixteen, had been staying with her for several months after English perpetrated an alleged assault.

Between 7:30 p.m. and 8:00 p.m., Officer Magill found English near his ex-girlfriend's aunt's home on Harvard Boulevard. Magill arrested the young man and placed him in the cruiser. English was compliant until Officer Magill took English inside the Montgomery County Jail and the latter head-butted the wall. Jail medics say English's pupils were not correctly dilated upon exam. Consequently, jail staff refused to process English without medical clearance. Unable to arrest English, Magill was told to take him to the hospital. At 8:45 p.m., Magill updated dispatch to report a change of transport for English.

"I'm going to be transporting him to Grandview Hospital for treatment of his injuries," Magill said. Magill drove English to Grandview Hospital for an evaluation. English was checked out and medically released. Before leaving the hospital, English asked Magill to use the phone since he was allowed one phone call.

Magill updated dispatch with the transfer of the young man back to jail. "537 Dispatch, transporting adult male to jail, again. Currently 67A," Magill said over the police radio. Magill and English, alone together, left Grandview Hospital around 9:35 p.m. English and Magill began conversing in the police cruiser. This time, Magill switched on the police cruiser's video surveillance camera.

"Kylen, just so you know, if you start acting goofy again, it's going to be on camera this time," Magill said. "I'd hate for you to have to pay for that medical bill."

"Do you believe you go to heaven if you kill yourself?" English asked him.

"Depends on what you believe in," Magill responded.

The next sound picked up by the cruiser's video camera was English hitting his head again, this time against the glass window. He repeatedly began bashing his head against the police cruiser window until the glass began to crack.

Magill pulls the cruiser over to the side of the road. "Hey, partner," he said.

When the car stopped, English uttered his last words. "I wanna die!" He continued banging his head against the glass until the window broke and kicked his way out. Once the car stopped, the glass shattered. Within a few seconds, English jumped out of the cruiser and over the side of the bridge.

Magill shouted, "Holy [expletive]!" Magill immediately called dispatch for a medial assist on Salem Avenue Bridge.

"Medic, my guy just jumped out my car window and hooked over the bridge," Magill called. "On Salem Street Bridge, uh, just north. I'm sorry, just north of Robert. It's going to be on the west side of the river. I'm sorry, east side of the river."

"Is he going to be in the water?" the dispatch operator responded. Magill peered down over the bridge where English had fallen.

"No, he's on the rocks," Magill answered.

"OK, we're going to get someone down here on the bike path—on the east side of the river right under the bridge," dispatch confirmed.

"The crews that are responding here, try and get someone on the bike path, if you can," Magill told the dispatcher. "I'm not sure where you get on. Try to drive down toward the south, north…however you get on." Frantic, unable to get to English, who was prone at the bottom of the bridge, Magill signaled dispatch to secure an emergency vehicle a second time. "537 dispatch. Do you have medics started this way?"

A few minutes went by. Other officers arrived at the Salem Avenue Bridge, including Police Lieutenant Kim Hill. "He head-dove out of the cruiser while in the middle of driving, got up again and jumped over the bridge like a no-hand swan dive," Magill informed the lieutenant. "My camera's on," Magill continued his verbal report to Lieutenant Hill and other attending officers. "I had just…I cuffed behind his back…BAM, BAM, he jumps out…Swan-dives over the bridge," Magill said. "He's right here, he's breathing…kind of. No hesitation. I mean, none."

Within thirty minutes, the ambulance arrived at Miami Valley Hospital on Wyoming Street. The coroner's report concluded that no gun wounds or Tasers were used against English. English's death, recorded at 10:21 p.m., was the direct result of his fall from Salem Avenue Bridge. Immediately, the community reacted with grief and despair. A young man lost his life while in police custody. The system had failed him.

"People were marching and coming to city commission meetings using their voices to call for accountability from the police," said Walrab.

A year later, in August 2012, the family filed a grievance against the police. The tensions seemed to be escalating day by day with no end in sight.

"There was no way to resolve other than fire the entire police staff or blow up the jail," Walrab said. "Thirty people came together in protest and created another voice. They made a statement to churches and came to the city commissioner and made a statement. The Dayton Mediation Center held twelve mediations, private and confidential. These meetings created an initiative between the police and community to build trust with the police."

In response to the community relations initiative, events began taking place at the Victoria Theater. This was a community in need of healing. Kids got together to read and write poetry about English's death and to speak about it. What came out of that was an initiative called Voice Kylen English. Four initiatives came out of the Kylen English story, which built trust between the Dayton African American community and the police department, while allowing young people to have a voice.

"This purpose seemed to stop the escalation of angst in our community and created a town hall activism between leaders and ordinary people just to talk to each other in private and say what they need to say," Walrab said. "Promises continued to be held." The Dayton community, the community leaders and the police got together to decipher what process was needed to bring peace and closure for this family. English's life was destroyed, and there was no bringing him back.

Dayton's Cityfolk, an arts group, has brought the best traditional artists from around the world to perform in concert, dance, festival and educational settings for over twenty years. Cityfolk initiated a low-budget music video released on YouTube in 2013, with half a million views or more, called, "Where There Is Love." The "Where There Is Love" video used eclectic globe-hopping imagery and sounds. The entire video was shot on-location at the edge of the Great Miami River downtown.

They invited conversation about Kylen English and put out a voice to the city of Dayton in talking to people and providing a platform for their voices to be heard down the road. This is a process that doesn't have a roof or an address. The initiative encouraged every person to come forward.

"The DMC holds five hundred to one thousand mediations per year with two to four thousand people a year," said Walrab. "After twenty-five years, roughly about 10 percent of the people of Dayton have been involved in mediation accumulatively. Over time, we have emerged as a community accustomed to sitting down and talking to each other under difficult circumstances." DMC customers in Montgomery County have emerged from conflict to become people who have participated in mediation and in group dialogue. People in connection to the DMC, which is supported by Montgomery County and by the City of Dayton, continue to use this practice to resolve conflict long after their cases are settled.

Transformative Mediation

Transformative Mediation, a methodology for conflict resolution, did not originate in Dayton, but it has garnered the DMC national attention from the successful integration of the program. The DMC transfers those same values to resolving conflict at low cost without legal implications. The center offers these self-management mediation services through both education and empowerment of citizens to create their own solutions, separate and apart from criminal liability. Clients served at the center are participants from non-criminal court cases, such as divorcing parents engaged in child custody squabbles, feuding neighbors or dissident co-workers. In a child custody battle, the parents are often pitted against each other in an adversarial position, which negatively affects the children. Child custody battles, or other civil and non-criminal cases traditionally fought out in court, are decriminalized in this type of conflict resolution and allow both sides to be heard and to heal.

The Dayton Mediation Center first opened in 1987 and began incorporating the transformative mediation model in 1998. Transformative mediation was first expounded on in 1994 by authors and researchers Robert A. Baruch Bush and Joseph P. Folger in the book *The Promise of Mediation.* This type of approach tends to destabilize the parties' experience of both self and the other so that the individuals interact in ways that are both more vulnerable and more self-actualizing than before the conflict. Without this approach, the negative dynamics often feed into each other or on all sides as the parties interact in a vicious circle that intensifies each party's distrust of the other(s).[26]

DMC receives an estimated 1,600 referrals a year, mostly submitted through the courts and the City of Dayton Police Department and all of which use about eighty community volunteers to resolve conflict and restore justice without the use of a moderator. As of 2013, the center has saved the Dayton community an estimated $650,000 in community resources since 1997. The mediation volunteers were trained at the DMC and have assisted mediations and three thousand Dayton citizens through 2014.

"The whole idea of community mediation is it's a grass-roots effort where citizens really come together to take care of their own problems and not have to rely on other services, like the police and the court system, to handle their conflicts," Michelle Zaremba, DMC director explained. The Juvenile Mediation Program was added to the roster of DMC services in July 1990, through cooperation with the Ohio Supreme Court, the Montgomery

The old Montgomery County Courthouse, on Third and Main Streets, in Dayton, Montgomery County, Ohio. Executions used to occur outside courthouse, which was constructed in 1850. *Courtesy of the Historic American Buildings Survey.*

County Juvenile Court and the Ohio Commission on Dispute Resolution for the purpose of reducing the recidivism rate for referred juvenile offenders.

In 2001, the DMC established a transformative peer mediation group with the Northmont School District first and branched out peer mediation training and conflict management services to the Dayton, Kettering, New Lebanon and New Carlisle School Districts. This program empowered school-aged children to participate in peer conflict mediation and in peer education on how to solve conflict. The DMC has successfully resolved a total of three hundred peer mediations between 2001 and 2013.

The center also offers customized resolution training, conflict management and systems design and team-building consultation for organizations and facilities. Restorative justice (also sometimes called reparative justice) focuses on the needs of the victims, the offenders and the community at large instead of simply satisfying legal claims and liabilities. Mediation works with offenders, victims and families to thwart repetitive offensive and criminal intent and establishes positive trends in round-robin discussions about the disciplinary action of a juvenile or a high-risk repeat offender.

Zaremba said the DMC provides:

> *1) Mediation that introduces conversation, as conflict mediation between conflicting parties, who previously may have not "felt heard" throughout court proceedings and litigation; 2) conflict coaching to participants who enter the conversation feeling frustrated, angry and under-valued and; 3) help to individuals to respond to conflict without escalating the issues at hand.*

Different types of mediation services are offered through the courts. DMC offers the Montgomery County Juvenile Court visitation mediation to resolve custody battles. In the Dayton Municipal Court, DMC offers several services: eviction mediation, Community Impact Panel and, lastly, provides court-ruled mandating mediation for civil cases.

As peer mediation evolved through the courts, the Adult Victim/Offender Program, offered through the City of Dayton's Prosecutor's Office and the Dayton Municipal Court Criminal Division, supported the growing endeavor for restorative justice beginning in 1999. The theory defines the mediator's goal as helping the parties to identify opportunities for empowerment and recognition shifts as they arise in the parties' conversation, to choose whether and how to act on these opportunities and, thus, to change their interaction from destructive to constructive.

8

MODERN-DAY PEACE ORGANIZATIONS

Dayton ensures peace through a living history. Dayton's Peace Accords heritage has extended beyond the community since the peace agreement was signed in December 1995. A few peace groups have led the movement in Dayton's modern peace legacy. Two longstanding city offices, the Human Relations Council and the Dayton Sister City Committee, a member of the Sister City International, invoked town hall meetings to make Dayton a more immigrant-friendly city. From that town hall meeting, a committee was created to form Welcome Dayton, an organization dedicated to Dayton's immigrant population. Other Dayton activists wanted to instill a culture of peace. Their mission activated other peace groups. The Greater Dayton Christian Coalition launched as many as forty community-wide events and organizations since the 1980s. A few activists started the Dayton International Peace Museum, which recognizes local and international peace heroes. A Dayton Literary Peace Prize, first honoring the work of Richard Holbrooke, was started in 2006. Many of these groups fought for civil rights and social justice for Dayton's diverse neighborhoods. Many just wanted to see a change and opened up with a community dialogue. And some found love.

Welcome Dayton

Dayton has been recognized by the White House Task Force on New Americans as a model of immigrant friendliness and integration. In April 2015, over a dozen initiatives across the Midwest launched Welcome Economies (WE) Global Network, a program that welcomes immigrants to America. The network is working to tap into the economic development opportunities created by attracting, welcoming and retaining immigrants.

"The city of Dayton is leaps and bounds ahead of other cities in peace building," said artist, activist and peace author J. Fred Arment. "This legacy started decades ago during the civil rights era." Dayton city committee members were appointed by the Dayton City Commission and the City of Dayton government on a volunteer basis for all activities undertaken on behalf of the Dayton Sister City Committee. Dayton was officially inaugurated as a member of Sister Cities International (SCI), created by President Eisenhower in 1956 in conjunction with a conference on citizen diplomacy.

The seven-story Neoclassical building of Dayton City Hall also doubled as the YMCA in 1908. *Courtesy of the Historic American Buildings Survey.*

The SCI's mission is to "promote peace through mutual respect, understanding, and cooperation—one individual, one community at a time." Dayton counts Agsburg, Germany; Oiso, Japan; Monrovia, Liberia; Holon, Israel; and Sarajevo, Bosnia, on its roster of sister cities. Sarajevo was added in 1999. Although the sister city program—held together by volunteers—was quite successful, most city-elected officials believed more was needed to ensure the rights of immigrants.

Tom Walrab, former director of the Human Relations Council (HRC), was among those who started Welcome Dayton. "The city of Dayton has gone through some changes in demographics since 2000," Walrab said. "Immigrants were buying houses in areas which had started to decay and were starting businesses. Many of the vacant, run-down, or abandoned buildings were purchased and fixed up, immediately raising property values."

The HRC saw a need to impress on the community that immigrants were assets to the region and were not depriving native-born Americans of employment and educational opportunities, which was often the misconception. Immigrants in Dayton were encouraged to seek help from the HRC and not to feel isolated. The City of Dayton Building houses the HRC on Third Street. The HRC has historically championed civil rights for women and minorities. According to Walrab, who was involved with mediation surrounding immigrants in 2009–10, multiple discrimination suits had been filed through the HRC.

Discrimination cases were brought up to the HRC because of employment and housing inequality. The Dayton Mediation Center, located in the same building as the HRC, was called in to mediate. Waldrab brainstormed with City of Dayton appointees Matt Joseph and Tim Reardon. Together, they spearheaded the effort to create Welcome Dayton. As a trained mediator volunteer, Walrab put out an invitation to the community and asked the city to join in and sponsor a dialogue.

The HRC represents the civil rights of minorities and immigrants worldwide. Welcome Dayton was added to augment these services as part of the same one-stop City of Dayton peace building in 2011.

"What does Dayton do best in a community crisis?" he asked. "We talked about it. People came out to talk about it. People volunteered to write the plan, and a committee came together to write a plan to add value or intentionally promote friendly services to immigrants." The community of Dayton took ninety days to write the plan for Welcome Dayton. While the plan was being written, the verbiage was available for anyone in the area to weigh in or to apply for any purpose promoting integration and efforts supporting immigration and Dayton immigrants.

"The Marion Schuster Center came forward and volunteered to sponsor yearly concerts featuring international music and made it free to any immigrant. Immigrants were also given a free pass to the Philharmonic Orchestra," said Walrab. "That is just one example of something the community stepped forward and did. Everyone took ownership and wrote part of the plan and became part of the solution. City government has hired someone to support it. The city manager and city commission office supported the initiative, and other community activists were anxious to be on the Welcome Dayton committee. The plan itself was endorsed by the city commission."

In 1999, among the aid sent to Bosnia in its reconstruction from the UN and other international peace-keeping coalitions, a scholarship program was set up for twelve students from Bosnia to take part in a student exchange program to study abroad in the United States. Two of the twelve students chose to attend school in Dayton because of the Peace Accords legacy. The other ten Bosnian students applied to study at other colleges in the United States.

One of the students who elected to attend college at the University of Dayton was Irena Karlovic Joseph. Irena came to Dayton in 1999 at the age of twenty through a fellowship grant. Many Bosnian refugees went to Germany and received some federal aid for political asylum in the years 1998 to 1999. Most were still leaving Bosnia and Herzegovina until that time.

"It was safe for the Bosniaks and the Croats then to travel about," Irena said. "The killing had stopped." The last known genocide of the Yugoslav wars, the Kosovo massacre of 1999, was over. And people began wanting to rebuild. Dayton was inducted as a new sister city of Sarajevo that same year and would become a permanent host city of peace and a reminder of what could be accomplished without gunfire. The UN characterizes peace as safety, prosperity and quality of life. Irena found something a little special in that quality of life in her student exchange studies that she hadn't imagined.

When the war escalated in Bosnia in 1992, Irena was thirteen years old. One by one, the countries in the Yugoslav territory began to secede, and the biased attacks against the minority ethnic groups surfaced in the media. Most of the ethnic groups in Bosnia before that time did not pay attention to the religion of the ethnic group they belonged to until the wars started and they were told they had to take sides. The Serbs objected to the secession and fought back with military assault and negative propaganda in the media. Irena's family was Christian, and although they were not persecuted as an ethnic group, her family did not feel safe. She and her family moved to a refugee camp in Croatia for two years.

"We were given false information and made to feel afraid of our neighbors because one side wanted to control what the entire country was doing," she said.

Irena said that, as a refugee, life was harsh. Refugees lose their homes, retirement, cash savings and livelihoods. The devastating effect is similar to someone battling a life-threatening illness without the benefit of health insurance.

"You didn't want to have to deal with it, but you do what you have to do," she said. "When countries started seceding in 1990 from the former territory of Yugoslavia, the monolithic Serbs didn't like it," she said. Ideally, the Yugoslav army didn't want the country to split, but the central government at Belgrade, a Serb majority, wanted the country united under Serb control. "People were forced to choose sides when they didn't want to," she said. People had not identified with an ethnic group, in many cases for centuries, but it was decided that they had to choose sides or be killed. There were many mixed marriages, and families lived in fear of being separated from their homelands or slaughtered."

In 1993, when she was fourteen, what she saw was that Croatians opened their homes and hotels to Muslim refugees who were endangered. After the war in Kosovo in 1999, the threat of slaughter had subsided in Bosnia, and it was safe for all to go back to their homes and families. She began her education in the United States at this time and wanted to return to Bosnia to make a difference in rebuilding the country.

Irena got involved in student government as a young girl and as a refugee because she saw, at a personal level, that many needed help with their English. America was the land of opportunity and spoke English almost exclusively, so she decided to teach English as a career choice. She moved back to Bosnia after completing her undergraduate education with the hopes of getting a job back home. However, she had already begun a correspondence with a future young Dayton city commissioner over the next four years that eventually blossomed into a courtship. Irena had no intention of staying in the United States as she furthered her studies until she met her future husband while still attending the University of Dayton, and they became friends.

"I didn't want to stay in the United States, but Matt was persistent," she said. The two didn't get married right away, and they were separated for four years while she was developing her career and completing her education. She moved to the United States in 2003 for the final time to finish her master's degree in language studies of Serbian and English at Wright State

University in 2004 and to marry Matt Joseph. Joseph was elected for his first term as city commissioner in 2004.

Irena returns to Bosnia every year to visit family for six or seven weeks. She stays in close contact with them and is teaching her two children to be bilingual. Employment and financial security is slowly beginning to improve back home. However, many middle-aged people who were in their prime during the war are struggling. They have no retirement, no benefits, no pensions and were unable to get loans. All purchases are made with cash only. Savings accounts dwindled for Irena's parents, as there were limited employment opportunities.

"No one at home [in Bosnia] knows how this war got started," she said. "If you ask, people will just shrug their shoulders." It was a war between neighbors, and it shouldn't have happened.

Commissioner Joseph has led citywide initiatives in promoting entrepreneurial enterprise, such as Tech Town, to make the city more attractive for young entrepreneurs. Joseph, a Lebanese immigrant's son, had a plan to make Dayton a more immigrant-friendly city. His father was an immigrant and had a strong entrepreneurial spirit. He started several businesses that put Joseph and his siblings through college.

"City leadership, from the city commissioner's office to the Dayton mayor, has traditionally stood behind the peace movement that led to the International Day of Peace," said Joseph. "Leadership was behind the DPA in 1995, and this legacy of peace building in Dayton stands today."

Although Irena made a smooth transition to the United States due to her command of the English language and customs, many did not. "Welcome Dayton is distinctly different because of how it came about," said Joseph. "Anybody and everybody was invited into a community-wide town hall meeting to discuss welcoming immigrants, and from that discussion, we wrote a plan. Immigration is the history of our country."

Welcome Dayton was started as an adjacent agency, empowered by the City of Dayton, to assist immigrants in smoothly transitioning to life in America. The Welcome Dayton committee created six focus areas to advocate for new immigrants: community, culture, business development, economic development, government and justice. The areas are considered collaborative and will intersect with other committees. "For example, there is the Dialogue Series which mirrors voices of the community. This is an opportunity to hear personal stories and bring a lot of value to change," said Waldrab. "This was a joint panel discussion between native-born Americans and immigrants. People share their stories over dinner and small group conversation."

The Peace Bridge

Another group promoting social justice and unity was started back in 1988. The people of East and West Dayton met at the intersecting bridge infrastructure that connects East and West Third Streets to celebrate integration and harmonious relationships between neighbors. Every year after that, the Peace Bridge Walk begins at the Peace Bridge, which is the same east-meets-west intersection on Third Street. The Peace Walk, hosted by the Greater Dayton Christian Connection and forty other local groups, has come to symbolize racial harmony in the city. Before desegregation ended in the 1970s, Dayton was divided between black and white, west and east.

The theme of the twenty-fourth-annual Peace Walk was "Lord, hear our cries." The Dayton Peace Bridge connection has evolved from a peaceful demonstration into an international proclamation of racial unity since Dayton's inception into the International Cities of Peace in 2010. "This is to show that we are one in sprit and action," said Reverend Crystal Williams, the Peace Walk coordinator since 2012. "As citizens of Dayton, regardless of skin color, we are called to act upon what we see are the different traumas and are not peaceful about Dayton."

To commemorate the twenty-fourth walk, which coincided with the 100th anniversary of the Dayton chapter of the NAACP, ten workshops relating to the violence that stems among race relations and immigration were planned. Activities celebrating interfaith connections, youth leadership development and added resources for the hungry and the homeless were procured.

The Dayton Christian Connection, which founded the group, pulled in organizations like the Baha'i to hold peace events, such as the International Day of Peace, the International Day of Prayer and the Dayton Dialogue on Race Relations. These events are devoted to civil rights actions and are trying to advocate for change against laws imposed on violence in Dayton, including the death penalty.

"We act upon what we see as traumas or not peaceful about Dayton," said Walker. "The Peace Bridge demonstration has become less about a march and more proactive as to how the city was going to come together to pursue peace in Dayton."

One activity is the International Day of Prayer held on May 7. On that day, the Baha'i Center hosts the one human family workshop as a member of the Greater Dayton Christian Coalition.

International Cities of Peace

"Counting Dayton, there are 110 International Cities of Peace around the world," said founding director J. Fred Arment. "These cities are committed to doing peace building within their communities. Each city has its own project. In Burundi, there are women who were raped and ostracized. The Cities of Peace Global Family Program helped fifty of them with housing and leases on gardens and school fees for the children. In the Democratic Republic of Congo, the network is helping to build a school that will educate over two hundred children made orphans by war.

"In our local city of peace, the PEACE DAYton group has grown by leaps and bounds," said Arment. "A peace cooperative of over sixty organizations, PEACE DAYton hosts nearly fifty events for the local celebration of International Day of Peace."

The Dayton International Peace Museum

After a visit to the Museum of the United States Air Force in 2003, green farmers Ralph and Christine Dull decided it was equitable to build a space for peace in the same city that had a museum in homage to war.

The Dayton International Peace Museum was the second peace museum of its kind to open in the United States. The Dayton International Peace Museum started out at the United Methodist Church near the Masonic Temple on Riverview, from 2003 to 2004. Then, it moved to its permanent home at the Pollack Mansion on Monument Avenue. The Pollack house, a historical mansion, was moved across town to its present and permanent address on Monument in 1979. The museum honors both Dayton's history as the center of the 1995 Dayton Peace Accords and its contribution to the international peace community. Ralph and Christine Dull, J. Frederick Arment, Lisa Wolters and Steve Fryburg founded the peace museum.

Ralph Dull is an Ohio farmer and a green energy specialist, and Christine is a former teacher. Both Christine and Ralph Dull are longtime peace activists and members of the Fellowship of Reconciliation. They received the 2009 Pioneer of Ohio Award from Green Energy Ohio and the National EPA Award for Environmental Stewardship in 2010. The Dulls are authors of the book *Soviet Laughter, Soviet Tears: An American Couple's Six-Month Adventure in a Ukrainian Village*. The Dulls traveled to work in the Union of the Soviet

Friends of the House of the People received the Dayton Peace Heroes Award given by the Dayton International Peace Museum. *Courtesy of Patsy Farrell, 2014.*

Socialist Republic (USSR) in 1989 with the goal of creating a friendship with the Soviet people. They were written up in *Time* magazine and the *New York Times*. Ralph's book *Nonviolence Is Not for Wimps: Musings of an Ohio Farmer* garnered international attention. Many people remember Christine's cello playing as a peaceful demonstration during the Dayton Peace Accords. The Dulls' work overseas outlines the basic strategies for modern nonviolent conflict resolution. J. Frederick Arment is an educator, marketing strategist and writer and founded International Cities of Peace, is facilitator for PEACE DAYton and is coordinating the Dayton Peace Trail. Arment is the author of two works of fiction, as well as two peace books, *The Elements of Peace: How Nonviolence Works* and *The Economics of Peace: Freedom, the Golden Rule and the Broadening of Prosperity*. Lisa Wolters is a graphic designer and a ceramic artist.

Fryburg, a writer, is a member of Veterans for Peace, a retired police officer and a museum curator for the Missing Peace Art Space in Dayton. As a former director of the Dayton International Peace Museum, Steve Fryburg said that, unfortunately, peace usually comes only after violence. From 2003 to 2005, the peace museum set up a mobile peace exhibit called the Peace Mobile in a van.

Volunteer committee members remember 9/11 at the Dayton International Peace Museum. *Courtesy of Patsy Ferrell, 2014.*

"Until 2003, there were no peace exhibits anywhere," said Fryburg. The first peace museum in the United States was started in Chicago but has since closed due to a lack of funding. However, the Dayton International Peace Museum had a few angel investors who donated money: the museum's founders and the architect of the Dayton Peace Accords. Ambassador Richard Holbrooke donated the $10,000 peace prize winnings to the museum after touring the van exhibit.

"True peace is proactive in its approach and preventative," he said.

The Dayton International Peace Museum is dedicated as a space for children and adults to find positive, nonviolent alternatives to a culture of violence. The peace museum serves not only as a traditional museum with peace exhibits but also as a meeting place for peace. The peace museum features permanent, temporary and traveling exhibits that highlight the rich history and potential of nonviolent solutions.

The educational programs and exhibits are nonpartisan and feature themes of nonviolent conflict resolution, social justice issues and international relations. The Peace Heroes Room on the second floor is a permanent multimedia interactive exhibit space devoted to well-known peace heroes, such as Mahatma Gandhi, and lesser-known ones, such as Ted Studebaker and Reverend Sister Dorothy Stang. In other annual celebrations of peace heroes, the museum selects and recognizes local peace heroes and holds a Nobel Peace Prize luncheon.

An agricultural worker and Christian Vietnamese peace volunteer, Studebaker was born in Dayton in 1945. He was killed on April 26, 1971, by North Vietnamese soldiers who attacked the volunteer's house with rockets and then invaded the structure. The soldiers did not know who Studebaker was. They merely saw him as an American and, therefore, a threat, so he was executed on the spot. His wife and the other volunteers were spared.

Sister Dorothy Stang, a human rights and environmental activist, was born in Dayton. She became a naturalized Brazilian citizen to advocate for her work for the rural poor of the country. Starting in the 1970s, Stang helped peasants earn a living by farming small plots and extracting forest products. In 2005, she was scheduled for a community meeting on the deforestation and preservation of the Amazon. She was stopped by two armed men, Clodoaldo Carlos Batista and Raifran das Neves Sales, who asked her if she had any weapons. Only a Bible, she said. She faced them as she read from the Beatitudes, "Blessed are the poor in spirit," from the New Testament book of Matthew. They fired six rounds into her body. Evan Mack composed an opera based on her life called *The Angel of the Amazon*.

Dayton Literary Peace Prize

The last Dayton Peace Prize was awarded in 2005 to Ambassador Richard Holbrook. The Dayton Literary Peace Prize replaced the Dayton Peace Prize in 2006.

"Press kits for the Dayton Literary Peace Prize have prizes listed for New York, D.C., Boston, Philly, Atlanta, Dayton, Chicago, L.A. and San Francisco," said Dayton Literary Peace Prize coordinator Sharon Rab. "Given the list of cities in that circle, the one that doesn't seem to belong is Dayton." However, the readership for peace-inspired literary works in Dayton is among the largest in the country. "Time after time, writers talk about what a terrific audience people in Dayton are. They actually read the books," said Rab.

Dayton's literary peace prize is the only literary peace prize in the United States and only one of three in the world. "There are two other literary peace awards, one in Canada, which is specific to Canadians," said Rab.

"The second—the Eric Remark Award—tends to favor German or other European writers."

"Lots of people give peace awards," said Rab. "We are the only literary peace prize. This is the perfect niche for Dayton." It was decided among the focus group that an annual literary peace prize in Dayton would keep it in the forefront of the peace movement.

"When we gave the last Dayton Peace Prize to Richard Holbrooke, he stood at the podium and said, 'Dayton should celebrate peace every year.'"

The Dayton Literary Peace Prize is awarded each year to three winning writers. The prizes are: the Richard Holbrooke Distinguished Achievement Award for lifetime peace achievement, a literary prize for nonfiction and a literary prize for fiction. After Holbrooke's passing, his widow, Katie, gave her permission to the committee to institute a lifetime literary achievement award in her husband's honor.

Since 2006, hundreds of publishing houses contribute authors for consideration. Nominees come from as far as Sri Lanka, New Zealand, Hungary, Singapore, South Africa, Australia, England and Canada. The Dayton Literary Peace Prize has become an annual international event.

A readership review committee selects one hundred nominations. "A group of first readers reads six books, and each book is read by three readers," said Rab. "All of the readers have some connection to Dayton, and range in age from twenty to eighty. They are from the politically left, middle, right. There are former generals, peace activists and university scholars."

Past winners encompass a range of established and emerging writers, including Karima Bennoune, Edwidge Danticat, Junot Diaz, Dave Eggers, Adam Hochschild, Marlon James, Adam Johnson, Andrew Krivak, Chang-Rae Lee, Francine Prose, Wilbert Rideau, Bob Shacochis and Andrew Solomon.

The Richard C. Holbrooke Distinguished Achievement Award is given to a writer for creating a lifetime body of outstanding literary contribution to peace. The Richard C. Holbrooke Award is given to peace writers who have created a distinctive footprint in literary peace. Past winners are Wendell Berry, Taylor Branch, Geraldine Brooks, Louise Erdrich, Barbara Kingsolver, Nicholas Kristof and Sheryl WuDunn, Tim O'Brien, Studs Terkel and Elie Wiesel.

While the many objectives in the Dayton peace groups may have divergent themes, the work is homogenized in perfecting peace processes. "So we choose our battles wisely. We do what we can. To engage, to connect, and to love is our greatest solace and our most powerful virtue," wrote author J. Frederick Arment.[27]

Appendix

DAYTON-AREA PEACE EVENTS

1815: The Warren County Peace Society established.

1915: The NAACP, Dayton chapter, established.

1995: The Dayton Peace Accords.

1995: Inception of Montgomery County's Job Center, the largest one-stop health, human services and workforce development system in the United States.

2000: The Dayton Peace Prize. The award was first given to William Jefferson Clinton.

2004 The Dayton International Peace Museum incorporated.

2005: The NAACP Youth Council.

2005: Ambassador Richard Holbrooke became the last recipient to win the Dayton Peace Prize.

2005: The Dayton Peace Accords 5K run. Friends and family participate in the scenic run for peace at the Dayton International Peace Museum for a peace-themed event.

2005: The martyrdom of Reverend Sister Dorothy Stang, formerly of Dayton.

2005: Council on Foreign Relations analysis on the Dayton Peace Talks.

2006: Dayton Literary Peace Prize established.

2009: International Cities of Peace established.

2010: Proclamation by Mayor Leitzell declaring Dayton a city of peace.

2010: The Salem Avenue Peace Corridor.

2013: PEACE DAYton established for the local celebration of International Day of Peace

2014: Nan Whaley and Mayor Rhine McLin reached out to the mayor of Sarajevo as a sister city on a mission of goodwill.

2015: The Five Rivers of Chautaqua of the Great Miami River Basin welcomed the nine traditional tribes of the Ohio region back to their native lands. The annual Pow Wow of the Five Rivers lasts for fifteen days and consists of traditional storytelling and dance.

2015: The First Annual Peace Heroes Walk. The Miami Valley honored peacemakers whose lives have inspired others to "be the change you wish to see in the world." Starting from Riverscape, downtown, the Peace Heroes Walk ends up at the front door of the Dayton International Peace Museum.

NOTES

Chapter 1

1. Ware, *History of Mechanicsburg*, 35.
2. Ohio Auditor of State's Office, "Office Publications."
3. Wilson, *Treaty of Greenville*, 22.
4. Holmes, *Dialogue on the Subject Slavery*, 2.
5. McDermott, *History of the First Presbyterian*, 52.
6. Ware, *History of Mechanicsburg*, 40–41.
7. Howe, *Historical Collections of Ohio*, 868.
8. Worcester, *Friend of Peace*, 32.
9. Dodge, *War Inconsistent with the Religion*, 5.

Chapter 3

10. Debrosse, "Film Snubs Ohio's Role Breaking the Enigma."
11. Debrosse and Burke, Secret in Building 26, 149.
12. Ibid., 73.

Chapter 4

13. Committee on the Remediation of Buried and Tank Waste, *Long-Term Institutional Management U.S. Department of Energy Legacy of Waste*, 122.

Chapter 5

14. Holbrooke, *To End a War*, 154.
15. Ibid., 23–24.
16. Ibid., 217.
17. Ibid., 204.
18. Ibid., 205.
19. Ibid., 307–9.

Chapter 6

20. Newsom, "May We Have This Dance?"
21. Newsom, "Thom, Ah-ee-la and Mahrah for All."
22. Newsom, "Perestroika."
23. Newsom, "Beat This."
24. Sidlow, "Searching for the Seoul of Dayton."
25. Navera, "Multicultural Dayton."

Chapter 7

26. Bush and Folger, *Promise of Mediation*.

Chapter 8

27. Arment, *Elements of Peace*.

BIBLIOGRAPHY

American Friends Service Committee. "An Introduction to AFSC's Work with Refugees in Dayton." http://www.afsc.org/video/introduction-afscs-work-refugees-dayton.

Arment, J.F. *The Elements of Peace: How Non-violence Works*. Jefferson, NC: McFarland & Co., 2012.

Atomic Heritage Foundation. www.atomicheritage.org.

Brooks, Nicholas. *To End All War*. Bloomington, IN: Iuniverse, 2014.

Bryant, Clifton D. *Handbook of Death and Dying*. Thousand Oaks, CA: Sage Publications, 2003.

Bush, B., and J. Folger. *The Promise of Mediation: Transformative Mediation Approach to Conflict*. San Francisco: Josey Bass Books, 2004.

Carson, Mary Kay. *Wright Brother for Kids: How They Invented the Airplane*. Chicago: Chicago Review Press, 2003.

Chollet, Derek, and Bennett Freeman. "The Secret History of Dayton: U.S. Diplomacy and the Bosnia Peace Process 1995." *National Security Archive*. http://www.gwu.edu/~nsarchiv/NSAEBB/NSAEBB171.

BIBLIOGRAPHY

CityFolk. "Where There Is Love: Playing for Change (HD)." https://www.youtube.com/watch?v=cABVKIPk_u0.

City of Dayton, Ohio. www.cityofdayton.org.

———. www.welcomedayton.org.

Coffin, Levi. *Reminiscences of Levi Coffin, the Reputed President of the Underground*. Cincinnati, OH: Robert Clark & Company, 1880.

Collins, Michael. *Flying to the Moon: An Astronaut's Story*. New York: Macmillan, 2011.

Committee on the Remediation of Buried and Tank Waste. *Long-Term Institutional Management U.S. Department of Energy Legacy of Waste*. Washington, D.C: National Academy Press, 2000.

Crouch, Tom D. *American National Biography*. New York: Oxford University Press, 1999.

———. *The Bishop Boys: The Life of Orville & Wilbur Wright*. New York: W.W. Morton Company, 1989.

Dayton International Peace Museum. www.daytonpeacemuseum.org.

Dayton Mediation Center. http://daytonmediationcenter.org.

Debrosse, Jim. "Film Snubs Ohio's Role Breaking the Enigma." *Cincinnati Enquirer*, January 14, 2015. https://www.cincinnati.com.

Debrosse, Jim, and C. Burke. *The Secret in Building 26*. New York: Random House, 2004.

Dodge, David Low. *War Inconsistent with the Religion of Jesus Christ*. Boston: International Union Ginn & Company, 1905.

Drury, Augustus Waldo. *History of City of Dayton and Montgomery County*. Vol. 1. Chicago: S.J. Clark & Company, 1909.

Feaster, Steven. "Women in Aviation." Special issue, *Business of Ohio* 4, no. 2 (2013): 117.

Final Impact Statement, Miamisburg, Mound Ohio. Washington, D.C.: U.S. Department of Energy, 1979.

Gallagher, Paul. "Neil Armstrong's Last Interview: Rare Glimpse of Man in Moon Mission." *Guardian*, May 24, 2012.

Gottfried, Ted. *The Liberation and Abuse of Holocaust Survivors*. Brookfield, CT: Twenty-first Century Books, 2001.

Greater Dayton Christian Connections. www.chritiansconnections.org.

Hannah, James. "Ohio Peace Museum Angling for Obama's Nobel Money." *Seattle Times*, October 2009.

Hasen, James. R. *First Man: The Life of Neil Armstrong*. New York: Simon & Schuster, 2005.

Heaton, Laura. "Trolander's Lifetime of Triumphs." *Yellow Springs (OH) News*, December 18, 2008. www.ysnews.com.

Heer, Fred J. *Ohio Archaeological and Historical Publications*. Vol. 9. Columbus, OH: Columbus Historical Society, 1905.

Holbrooke, Richard. *To End a War*. New York: Random House Publishing Group, 2011.

Holmes, Daniel. *Dialogue on the Subject Slavery and Other Subjects by the Word of God*. Dayton, OH: Gazette Books, 1854.

Howe, Henry. *Historical Collections of Ohio*. Cincinnati, OH: C.H. Krehbiel & Company, 1908.

Intellectual Reserve, Inc. "Ohio Archives and Libraries." *Church of Jesus Christ of Latter-Day Saints*. https://familysearch.org/learn/wiki/en/Ohio_Archives_and_Libraries#Archives.

International Cities of Peace, Inc. www.internationalcitiesofpeace.org.

Johnston, J., S. Armrhein and R. Thompson. "Neil Armstrong: Reluctant Hero." *Cincinnati Enquirer*, July 1999.

Kaplan, Robert D. *Balkan Ghosts: A Journey Through History*. New York: St. Martin's Press, 1993.

Keifer, Artimus. *Geography of Ohio*. Kent, OH: Kent State University Press, 1996.

Kern, Kevin. F. *Ohio History of the Buckeye State*. Malden, MA: Wiley & Sons, 2014.

Lee, Barbara. http://lee.house.gov.

Library of Congress. "H.R. 808—Department of Peacebuilding Act of 2013." https://www.congress.gov/bill/113th-congress/house-bill/808.

Lomask, Milton. *Invention and Technology*. New York: Simon & Schuster, 1991.

Lorcachi, Constantin. *Transforming Peasants, Property, and Power: The Collectivization of Romania*. New York: Central European Press, 2009.

McDermott, Clark. *A History of the First Presbyterian Church in Dayton, Ohio*. Dayton, OH: Henry L. Brown, 1880.

Mennonite Church USA. "Who We Are: A Quick Visual Guide." http://www.mennoniteusa.org/about-us/who-are-the-mennonites.

Navera, Tristan. "Multicultural Dayton: Dr. Chandan Gupta, Family Medicine Physician." *Dayton (OH) Business Journal*, May 8, 2014.

Newsom, Tammy. "Beat This." *Dayton City (OH) Paper*, November 18, 2014. www.daytoncitypaper.com.

———. "May We Have This Dance?" *Dayton City (OH) Paper*, October 14, 2014. www.daytoncitypaper.com.

———. "Perestroika." *Dayton City (OH) Paper*, May 6, 2014. www.daytoncitypaper.com.

———. "Thom, Ah-ee-la and Mahrah for All." *Dayton City (OH) Paper*, August 19, 2014. www.daytoncitypaper.com.

Ohio Auditor of State's Office. "Office Publications." https://ohioauditor.gov/publications.html.

Ohio History Central. "Dayton, Ohio." *Ohio History Connection*. http://www.ohiohistorycentral.org/w/Dayton,_Ohio.

Ohiomeansjobs.com. www.ohiomeansjobs.com.

Open Congress. "Bills." https://www.opencongress.org/bill.

PACO Dayton. http://www.pacodayton.org.

Peace Alliance. www.peacealliance.org.

Perkins, James. *Annals of the West: Embracing a Concise Account of Events*. St. Louis: James R. Albach, 1851.

The Promised Land: Ethnic Groups in the Valley. Dayton, OH: Gem City Savings Association, 1974.

Rouscup, Edwin. "The Baha'i Community of Dayton." Master's thesis, Wright State University, Dayton, OH, 1977.

Schonberg, Maria. *Heinman State Studies: The People of Ohio*. Chicago: Capstone Global Library, 2003.

Sealander, Judith. *Grand Plans: Business Progressivism and Social Change in Ohio's Miami Valley, 1890–1929*. Lexington: University Press of Kentucky, 1988.

Sidlow, Sarah. "Searching for the Seoul of Dayton." *Dayton City (OH) Paper*, January 28, 2014. www.daytoncitypaper.com.

Siebert, William Henry. *The Underground Railroad: From Slavery to Freedom*. New York: Macmillan & Company, 1899.

Skarup, Harold. *Ohio Warbird Survivors*. Lincoln, NE: Iuniverse, 2003.

Walvin, James. "Murdering Men." *Black Ivory: Slavery in the British Empire.* 2nd ed. Malden, MA: Blackwell Publishers, 2001.

Ware, Joseph P. *History of Mechanicsburg.* Columbus, OH: F.J. Heer Printing, 1917.

Wilmington College. http://www.wilmington.edu.

Wilson, Frazer. *The Treaty of Greenville.* Piqua, OH: Correspondence Press, 1894.

Worcester, Noah. *Friend of Peace.* Cincinnati, OH: William & Mason, 1817.

Wright Stories. http://wrightstories.com.

INDEX

X

Y

Z

ABOUT THE AUTHOR

Dayton native Tammy Newsom comes from a public service background with a concentration in sales and recruiting. She has been published as a freelance writer since the early 2000s and has written numerous news articles with the *Dayton City Paper*, the *Dayton Daily News* and *Impact Weekly*. Tammy is employed with the Montgomery County Job and Family Services. She has a bachelor of fine arts degree in drama from the University of Cincinnati.